Friendship—Bread for the Journey

Friendship—Bread for the Journey

Reflections edited by Doris S. Platt

Perfect Niche Publishing
Scottsdale, AZ

Perfect Niche Publishing
An imprint of Poisoned Pen Press
6962 E. 1st. Ave. #103
Scottsdale, AZ 85251
info@perfectniche.com

Printed in the United States of America

To my friends, whose companionship enriches and sustains me.

Acknowledgment

In a world where so many issues and problems divide us, I wanted to do something that would reflect how much we have in common. My gratitude to all those who responded so generously. Your words have come from the heart and deserve to be savored.

A waitress in a busy restaurant hurriedly put an overflowing mug of hot chocolate in front of me.

"I'm sorry," she said. "We didn't have a cup big enough to hold it."

Little did she know that her comment was a fitting conclusion to the day. With stories to tell and time to tell them, a friend and I had driven through a landscape awesome in its majesty and variety. The trip had taken us to Arches National Park in Utah. In this region of sculpted earth and red stone millions of years in the making, a sign on a marked trail caught my eye: "Fiery Furnace — Hiking Permit Required." A nearby notice urged visitors to travel in the company of others. The terrain was rough, and the warning had obviously been made for reasons of safety.

Rough terrain or smooth, who better to journey with us than a friend? A friend is a companion, "one with whom we have shared bread." Both bread and friendship bring nourishment; both are universal to the world.

In friendship's generous choreography of give-and-take, we offer who and what we are. We gain strength from its consistency and bask in the warmth of its acceptance. Now and then this relationship of choice is given to us fully formed; more often, it is woven slowly through generosity of trust and time.

Sleep deprivation did funny things to my mind. Black rings obscured my vision. I alternated between crying and laughing. Nausea and lethargy were sandbags around me and I could not make a decision. It was not until sheer exhaustion drove me to the very brink that I learned the value of sacrifice.

Service, unselfishness; these were both points of satisfaction I thought I had transferred from Sunday school to life, but it took the sacrifice of a remarkable woman to teach me about friendship.

After nine very difficult months of pregnancy I gave birth to my first child, a very hungry girl. As a new mother I wanted to give her the best and nurse. Specialists had warned me against supplementing feedings because it would create confusion.

The next time an expert gives me advice that flies in the face of the obvious, I will throw it out the window. Nevertheless, I followed that advice with disastrous consequences. My baby lost weight, cried constantly, and slept in hour-long intervals.

At two months, she was foundering and I was near exhaustion. All the symptoms of sleep deprivation combined with serious postpartum depression to make me one of those hysterical moms you read about in the news who do something terrible to their children. I needed help. My husband was holding down long hours at work and despite valiant efforts to lend a hand, was also unable to care for this screaming baby of ours.

On the telephone I cried out my heart to my dear friend Stephanie who was nursing her own baby. She offered to give me six hours of time off. The tone of my voice must have scared her because she promised to

1

make the twenty mile drive that very evening.

I protested that she could not leave her own two children. Trapped in my situation, I irrationally thought no one could possibly help me. She calmly told me her baby would not die if she was gone for six hours. Then she reassured me my baby would not die either. She arrived with a smile and took my infant from my shaking arms. Knowing my girl was in good hands, I finally slept.

Six hours later I awakened as someone who had been made whole. I felt like me again for the first time in months. After hours of hungry cries Stephanie had logically given my baby a bottle. I heard nothing. She had unplugged the phone, closed the door and gave me the very thing I needed most: sleep. Such a simple gift to give, but therein was the lesson I learned. Friends get to peek in the window at your private moments of hell and give you gifts you really need, not just the things they feel like giving. Like a sister, my friend dealt with the unpleasantness of a crying baby, and knew it was temporary. The impact of her gift was long-lasting.

Renewed with a breath of sanity, I was able to continue. My sweet child responded to Mommy's new inner peace and slept more. I slept more. Stephanie will probably never know the crisis she averted, but I will never forget. When I was really tired my friend let me sleep.

Past friendships are history.
Future friendships are a mystery.
Today's friendships are a gift.
That's why we call today the present.

Making friendships is like a seed planted in good earth. One needs to nourish and cultivate that relationship for it to grow. Once grown and strong it can withstand hard times and will never die.

3

ABBIE VIANES
SENIOR EXECUTIVE DIRECTOR, GOVERNOR'S COMMISSION ON WOMEN AND FAMILIES

Friendship is a soul connection of kindred spirits. My life entwined with another's for some time in a pure friendship untainted by agendas, unfettered by past baggage or future expectations and simplified because there were no male-female tensions. It was a pure laboratory of friendship for learning the deeper lessons which have blessed each subsequent relationship. For the first time in my life, I felt a deep desire to do no harm, to be careful in my words, to go back and clarify my intent and to ensure that my assumptions were correct. I discovered why people share their soul thoughts—to create a connection and to hopefully help one another through their experiences. I had never had an opportunity like this—such a pure playing field for practicing relationship skills.

The most impactful lesson I learned was that in order for friendship to flourish, both parties must be willing and capable of a sequence of attributes: It begins with humility—both must be able to come to each other and admit their wrongdoings, wrong sayings, wrong not doings and not sayings! Then there must be dialogue—open, non defensive, non attacking, simply talking it out to arrive at understanding. Forgiveness is next, which means no bringing it up again in a later dispute—it was laid to

4

rest. The result of this sequence—humility to dialogue to forgiveness—is resolution. The relationship conduit remains clear. It does not become clogged or choked with unresolved misunderstandings and hurts.

Friends protect each other, emotionally as well as physically. Thoreau aptly said that "friends cherish each other's hopes; they are kind to each other's dreams." Friends motivate, support, encourage. Most of all, they know how to listen and simply be there.

"Friendship enables you to step off the stage of life, take off your mask and be yourself in good and bad times."

"Friendship is respecting who you are, not what you are."

"Friendship is about trust, love, laughter, sharing, forgiveness, understanding, compassion, tolerance, shared experiences."

"Friendship goes beyond 'doing'—it is more about 'being'."

"Friendship is the 3 C's: Commitment, Communication, Companionship."

"A friend is a part of yourself."

"A friend is a person you respect and care for at the same time."

"A good friend sharpens your character, draws your soul into the light and challenges your heart to love in the greatest of ways."

"A friend tells you the truth—even if you do not like it."

"Friendship means sharing openly; trusting always, caring deeply."

"Friendship requires equality and loyalty."

"When the rest of the world lets you down a friend will find a tiny blue spot for you in the cloudy sky."

I could not live without friends. They have given meaning to my life and I realize now how much I have learned from my friends, especially those whom I admire.

I think we all have experienced the wonderful feeling of having friends over a long span of years with large gaps of passing before seeing them again. And yet when we meet we take up the conversation without missing a beat. We are in tune and have always cared about the same things.

I cherish my friends and what they have taught me. Many have passed on but I think often of what they meant to me in my life.

There was a woman pediatrician who had polio from the age of seven and wore braces on her legs until she died in her mid-eighties. She was the soul of personal courage, dedication to good medicine, compassion, and despite all had a *joie de vivre*. She loved the arts, good books, good music and made friends in her many travels to far off places in the cause of medicine, especially for children.

Another friend I cherish was a woman doctor who was born in Vienna and fled to America to escape the Hitlerian anti-Jewish horror. She was the epitome of courage and had a brilliant mind. She stood strong in the things that counted even if it would have helped her to play along. She was meticulous in her work as a medical librarian and a great cellist.

Other friends who fall into that special category are some of the newspaper women I knew. One of them was my roommate, a fine reporter with an inquiring mind and a great lover of nature. She opened my eyes to the green world around me.

Another friend was a college buddy

who later taught literature at the University in Chicago. She was magnificent in her knowledge of the English poets in the Victorian era. She also was an expert on Gilbert and Sullivan. We were lifelong friends.

Another woman, who was a fashion editor of the Washington newspaper, was a great friend. We were simpatico in all things and her sense of humor was a joy. She was of Greek heritage and we loved to go to Greek affairs where the music and dancing transformed our lives.

I have many men friends who also paved the way to more learning, greater knowledge especially in journalism and world politics.

Friends are indispensable. They are there when you need them. No questions asked. Their love is unconditional once you have established that you too feel the same way about a friend.

I have been lucky to have good friends and they have made my life so much better.

No man is an island.

Throughout my life I've been blessed with wonderful friends. People who welcome me into their homes and visit mine. Who are always there for me and know that I, too, am there for them. People with whom I can laugh, or cry, or be silent. In whom I can confide my fears, with whom I can discuss exciting ideas. Friends. We trust, and respect, and love each other.

I can still remember, when I went to a new school, how lonely I was before I found a special friend, when there was no one to giggle with, to confide in, to share jokes with, to plan escapades with. What a difference it made, when Clo (Marie Claude) came into my life and we teamed up to enjoy the present and dream about our futures.

If Clo and I had not forged that friendship among the desks and ink, my African dream might never have materialized. At least it would have been at a different time and, perhaps, taken a different form. It was Clo who wrote and invited me for a holiday in Kenya, five years after we left school.

Looking back over the 70 years of my life I realize that certain individuals stand out as 'super friends,' and chief among these was my mother, Vanne (pronounced 'Van'). Of course, our relationship began as a typical (or perhaps not so typical) mother-child relationship. But as I matured, so did the bond between us. It was she who supported my childhood dream of going to Africa to live with wild animals and write books about them.

It was she who volunteered to accompany me to the forests of Gambia National Park in Tanzania when I was offered the opportunity to study wild chimpanzees. This was because the authorities of what was

9

then the British Protectorate of Tanzania refused permission for a young girl to go into the field on her own.

Vanne stayed with me for four months, by which time everyone realized that I'd be okay on my own. With Vanne I shared the frustrations of the early weeks when the chimpanzees repeatedly fled at the sight of the strange white ape in their midst. With Vanne I shared the excitement of each new discovery.

As the years rolled by, it was Vanne who provided support whenever the going got tough, with whom I discussed every problem, every success. And so it continued until her death three years ago. She was 94, and had been my best friend for 67 years. Her passing left a void that can never be filled.

One other 'super friend' of my childhood was Rusty. He was a medium-sized black dog, whose coat gleamed copper in the sunlight.

His parentage was uncertain, his influence exceptional, his personality unforgettable. He accompanied me everywhere dogs were permitted—and many where they were not. He taught me the meaning of unconditional love and loyalty. He was sensitive to every shift of my mood. He demonstrated—when I returned, after an absence, or announced "Walkies!"—pure, uncontrived joy. Not without reason has the dog been described as 'Man's best friend.'

When I began my chimpanzee study I soon realized that friendships were important in the chimpanzee world. David Greybeard was the first individual to lose his fear of me. His close companion was Goliath, the top ranking male of the community. The two often traveled together and spent hours grooming each other. Sometimes I saw them playing, laughing and chasing around a tangle of vegetation. Goliath hurried to support David if he was in trouble, and David, not surprisingly, was more confident when Goliath was part of his group. What was interesting was that Goliath was clearly more relaxed, and better able to stand up to a challenge from the other males when he was with David. Over the years we have observed many other such friendships, especially between adult males. These close relationships endure over time, and are very different from the temporary alliances often formed between two individuals when each is trying to advance his own position in the hierarchy. They are very political animals!

I know of many strange friendships in the animal world. Particularly moving is the story of the abandoned, starving kitten who has become the inseparable companion of an orphan Grizzly bear. 'Cat' (as she was subsequently named) evaded all attempts to capture her by the staff of a wild-life refuge in Oregon.

One morning the emaciated kitten went into the enclosure where two-year-old Grizz was eating his breakfast. Those watching expected to witness a sudden ending of her short life. To their astonishment, the bear nudged a morsel of meat from his meal towards the kitten, and watched benignly as she devoured it. From that moment on Cat and Grizz have been inseparable. Grizz shares all his meals. And the two play together and sleep together, the little cat curled up close to her huge friend and protector.

There is one other inspiring friendship I must describe. It is the story of two Jack Russell puppies that were found huddled together, terrified, and covered with blood. They were taken to a humane shelter where the staff found that one of them had been repeatedly stabbed in both eyes. He was quite blind. After a few days, when his terrible wounds were beginning to heal, he was reunited with his companion. To the wonderment of the staff, the seeing dog took it upon himself not only to protect his blind friend, but to guide him around their enclosure, to the food and water bowls, to their bed, and to greet those who came to visit.

The two were found a home where they could stay together and, with the constant help of the seeing companion, the blind youngster would soon find his way around in their new surroundings. They are together still.

In the Bible Jesus says, "Greater love hath no man than he who lays down his life for a friend." History is filled with inspiring examples of heroic friendships, personal courage and sacrifice. And in everyday life the value of friendship is driven home again and again, as friends help each other through a variety of personal tragedies and crises, providing help, advice, a sympathetic ear. Offering love and, above all, loyalty.

These days I travel three hundred days a year, raising awareness of environmental and social injustices, and raising funds for new projects. I could not survive this hectic schedule if it were not for the support and love of the many wonderful friends I have in so many parts of the world. Friends with whom I can relax and in whom I can confide. With whom I can enjoy a glass of red wine and a simple meal. With whom I can share a good laugh. Indeed, true friendship is one of the greatest blessings in our lives.

As I think about friends, I must include my husband and children as my closest friends. However, there have been others over the years who influenced and helped me. I am a private person who does not open up freely to other people so I have not had many really close friends, but I appreciate those who have accepted me.

Recently I have been thinking about two very special people from long ago high school days. Although our paths have seldom crossed in the years since we left our youth, I remain grateful for their friendship.

Having been born shortly before World War II began and being an American of Japanese ancestry, the war affected me deeply. My family was living on the West Coast of California when President Roosevelt signed an order after Pearl Harbor was bombed that all those of Japanese ancestry living on the West Coast of the United States should be locked up in hastily constructed camps in remote, undesirable areas. Although we avoided being incarcerated in an internment camp, as were many of our fellow Japanese-Americans, we lost almost everything and were uprooted from our home.

My father had been born in Japan, came to the United States as a young man, and was running a successful produce business in Southern California. My mother was born in America but had spent the years between the ages of twelve and eighteen living in Japan with relatives after her mother had passed away.

My older brother and I lived a comfortable existence with our parents in the Los Angeles area. With the outbreak of war in December 1941, all that changed and life became uncertain. We were renting a small but nice home in Los Angeles, the business

13

was going well, we had friends close by, and life was basically good. With the notice that evacuation and the incarceration of the Japanese-Americans was imminent, my parents made arrangements with relatives in Utah to move there slightly ahead of the order to enter the camps. Permission was granted, possessions **were** disposed of quickly at great loss, the truck used in the produce business was loaded with remaining essential items, and our family of four with another one on the way began a different life.

I was a small child and do not remember the events of that time, but I do recall the end of the war and the persecution and name-calling that ensued. I believe those experiences made me apprehensive each time I have subsequently made a change in living arrangements and been required to make new friends. There were several moves during the years that followed as my father tried to eke out a living for the family mostly by doing truck farming on a small-scale.

In the fourth grade I met two fellow students, Nancy and Maria. They remained my closest friends during the joys and the sometimes troubling and difficult years of high school.

Nancy is Caucasian. Maria is Mexican-American, and I am Japanese-American. Though from very different backgrounds, the three of us were inseparable. We had many experiences and did many things together, but mostly we just enjoyed the day-today activities of living and growing up. People called us the Three Musketeers because we were together constantly.

We did not talk about our ethnicity or differences, but having Nancy and Maria accept me for who I was, in spite of my failures and shortcomings, helped me greatly.

Because of my witnessing and experiencing discrimination and sometimes overt racism as I grew up, I did not have the best self-esteem and was often apprehensive in new situations. These two friends helped bring meaning into my life. Their friendship has meant much to me over the years although I have not really expressed these feelings to them. I will always be grateful to Nancy and Maria for being my friends as I am grateful for those who are my friends now.

Measures and measurements, fixed by law or custom, differ greatly from one region of the world to another.

In English-speaking countries, shoe sizes are reckoned by an old measure called the barleycorn, which is equal to a third of an inch.

The ancient Chinese had an uphill mile and a downhill mile. Because it takes more energy to walk uphill than downhill, they made the uphill mile shorter.

A scruple was an ancient Roman coin, its worth determined by its weight in gold. Although these standards are many and varied; the value we place on friendship is universal. People of divergent backgrounds and nationalities find that this gift lies closest to the heart.

DSP

16

Friendship is composed of more than one note. The wise among us accept people by content of character.

I remember in the 1970s when I was at sea in an oil tanker in the Pacific and Far East. There was an Indian man who befriended me. I was the engineer, and it was his job to check out oil and water levels and generally clean up. He did far more than that; he looked after me as a friend.

I never picked up a tool but he was there to give me a hand. If he thought I was overworking he was at me to take a rest while he carried on. One time in particular we had a main steam pipe blow out on us. Everybody had to evacuate the engine room. I foolishly went to shut the valves and passed out. My friend came in through another doorway to the engine room and dragged me out. He saved my life.

When we went ashore in Thailand, Singapore, even up to Saigon, he brought fresh fruit for me, to make sure I ate properly. When we were at sea again, he would come down to the engine room with glasses of ice-cold coconut milk, because I did not drink tea. At no time did he look for anything in return except my well-being.

We used to go into Bombay for crew changes and the shipping agent would come on board. I tried very hard to have my friend promoted as he surely deserved it—he was better than the junior engineer I had at the time, but the authorities would not entertain the idea because of his caste.

I used to sunbathe and he kidded me about trying to become as black as he was. He would ask me did I think that if he went up on deck and sat in the moonlight, would he become a white man!

17

I never met a better or more genuine person. He taught me a lesson that true friendship is above material things of this world, above even the ability to speak more than a handful of words in the same language. There are no barriers of race, creed or culture to friends.

I have made some amazing friends in a most unexpected place. I frequent a home and gardening site on the Internet, and have found some of my very closest friends there. Some of us have met in person; some of us have spoken on the phone. We write letters, send packages, give each other cyber-hugs and prayers when needed, cheer when things go well, and share sadness when something doesn't work out.

The most amazing thing I have been involved in with this group of people happened a few Christmases ago. One of the members of the site had lost most of her possessions in a house fire. Yet when people were talking on the discussion boards about their Christmas trees, holiday ornaments, etc., she was just as excited as the rest of us to hear about them.

Then someone had the idea of having an ornament exchange, and to make this particular woman the recipient. We as a group were from all over the globe, various countries, states, provinces. We sent her ornaments that meant something to us personally, represented some aspect of our lives, our homes, something meaningful.

Because of the worries about the safety of the Internet and giving out too much personal information, her pastor agreed to her using the church's address, and was overwhelmed with the response. I believe she received over one hundred ornaments. She would update us every few days as to what had arrived in her mail. There were many smiles, and many happy tears were shed reading these descriptions. I'll never forget the way our Internet community pulled together. We as the givers gained much more than we could ever have given to her. Friends can be found in the most unexpected places.

19

My family moved from the city to the country when I was nine years old. I was devastated. I had just finished 3rd grade and had worked very hard to be one of the popular "cool" kids. The FOR SALE sign went up in June, and by August we were moving. My popular "cool" friends would come over every day during those two months and we would cry together and make plans to visit each other. The date finally came when I had to say goodbye to them and I was miserable.

School began a few weeks after we moved and that started the devastation all over again. I was very shy in new situations and walking into my 4th grade class was sheer terror. I went immediately to the back of the room and sat in the last desk in the last row. I didn't want anyone to speak to me. I looked around at the other kids coming back from vacation, renewing old friendships and catching up on everyone's summer activities. There was an excitement in the room, but not as far as I was concerned, and I slumped down even farther in my chair.

As I was sitting there observing the activities of the classroom, I saw a girl walking toward me. I tried to look invisible, but apparently I didn't succeed—she still saw me. She came right over to me and said, "Hi, are you new here?" I answered in the affirmative, and she planted herself at the desk next to mine and said, "My name is Edith, and I'll show you around." It surprised me, but I actually felt a little better. She started pointing people out, told me their names, where they lived, and shared a whole list of worthless information that was beginning to mean something to me.

By the time lunch rolled around,

Edith and I were glued at the hip. She had introduced me around and I was beginning to feel better about being there. She was there for me during school and she was showing me around after school.

After a week or two, I realized that Edith was pretty low on the totem pole as far as popularity goes. By that time it was pretty easy for me to make friends with the "cooler" kids, but my ticket into that group was to get rid of Edith. So I did the only thing a formerly popular nine-year-old could do—I ditched her.

Life went on and I never looked in Edith's direction again. It's been thirty-six years and I have had many friends and acquaintances whose names I can't remember. I have thought of her occasionally over the years wishing I had thanked her for her friendship, but never did. She extended herself to a stranger, made a difference in that person's life, and never got anything in return. I'm sure she has no memory of me, but her name will always stay in my mind, because for two weeks of my life she was my best friend.

Just in front of my computer screen is a miniature reproduction of a road sign for Exit 45A: Down East and Acadia Region.

This is a souvenir that a friend sent me; one of the things we have in common is a connection with Mount Desert Island. My office is in London, England, thousands of miles from Maine, but I often look at it when I feel a bit lost in life.

I rely on my friends to tell me when I'm off course. But also know that often they have maps of where they have been that I haven't visited yet, and if I find myself in unfamiliar territory I can ask them for guidance.

It is with utter humility that I write this story for you. Not because I want to tell it as much as the story wants to be told. I am humbled to be asked, because I did not experience true friendship till I was an adult.

My childhood was one of neglect and pain. My family looked okay to the outside world, but in truth we were in confusion and falsehoods difficult to comprehend.

The family was made up of my older brother, me and my younger sister. Of the three of us I was the only one with blue eyes like my mother, and I was the one who stayed with my mom as her 'helper' at the young age of two when she suffered a life changing stroke. I was the "good girl," useful and attempting to please. I always wanted to make the way better. We grew up, like weeds, and when the time for college came my brother went away. My sister also went to

college. I, however, was very sick at the end of my senior year. And while I was accepted at a college, my health was poor and I had no money for higher studies, so I worked for a while as a Sears catalogue salesgirl and then at a meat market, making prepared products like hot dogs and sausages.

My family encouraged me to further my education, but I was sure I would fail so I never tried. Through the efforts of my mother and an aunt, I was offered a job near my hometown, at an Outdoor Education Camp, where classes of elementary students came to stay for a week to learn about our natural world. My mother was an unofficial bird and flower expert in our town; that and the great gift of observation she had passed on to us children were my only qualifications for this new job as assistant to the teaching staff. That job and the people I met there

23

were to take my life in a direction I could never have imagined.

One day as I drove to the camp, I noticed a young, athletic looking women walking in the same direction. I slowed down to offer her a ride, but she cheerily waved me on with a nod of thanks. I could not have known then this person would change my life, my destiny forever.

Miriam is this woman's name and that day was thirty-five years ago and we are still friends. I worked with Miriam as an assistant on a rotating schedule about once a month. We had a lot in common as teacher and assistant. She shared her teaching skills; I shared my inherited knowledge and love of the local flora, fauna, geology and history. I took her to meet my family as she was from New York.

We enjoyed staff outings together, and as time rolled by I was given more responsibility. For the first time in my life I was more than accepted, I was appreciated for my intrinsic, formerly unnoticed skills and talents. I discovered through Miriam and the other teachers and staff, that I, in fact, did have something to offer the world. I had wanted to be a teacher like my mom and my aunt, but because I did not feel I was college material, I had given up that hope until I found that in this setting, I did have teaching skills and experience that could be useful.

At the end of that year Miriam was married and followed her new husband to Fairbanks, Alaska where he was enrolled at the University. We stayed in touch. Miriam shared her new experiences in great detail and I kept her up-to-date with all the camp happenings. That winter of 1970 she invited me to come visit their tiny little cabin in the woods outside Fairbanks. So the following June, with a job still waiting at camp when I came back from my visit, I took off, hitchhiking from Michigan to Alaska.

The friends I met along the way are another group of stories, amazing stories, as is that journey across America and Canada, but I will finish this one by saying this: Miriam and her husband took me in, made me feel more welcome than my own family ever has. And I loved Alaska, her majestic beauty, her incredible, real people and the freedom of experiences that challenge all those who live in this wild land. I found my true home. And this is where I have lived and grown and raised a son. I know there is a Higher Power who blesses all of us in an infinite wisdom we can only know as Grace.

I give credit to Miriam and her generous gift of friendship. I honor her for her authentic humanity and her compassionate friendship. From Miriam, I learned about friendship and the unexpected way a chance meeting can change a person's life and destiny.

Oh yes, I have friends. You can't ever have too many. My best friend and I met in Kindergarten. We grew up in the same neighborhood and stayed in touch even after both our families moved to other parts of town. It wasn't all that easy to do because we were only kids then.

I was just thinking about her because later today we're going to a show together. We can talk about anything. I trust her because she knows how to keep a confidence. She tells me the truth when some people might be afraid in case they would lose the friendship.

26

Friendship eases the pain of our lonely hearts, closes its eyes on our weaknesses, and gives the sweet and calm assurance that we are not alone in our journey through life. It lightens our burdens; infuses our hearts with hope as it cleanses them from selfishness; and turns us from being "strangers in a strange land" to a band of brothers. It binds our souls to those of others and, by opening our hearts, permits us to reach beyond the self-absorption of the natural man.

It calls us to see all men and women everywhere as our brothers and sisters. Its highest expression is found in voluntary service to others, in recognition of the Apostle Paul's assertion that God "hath made of one blood all nations of men for to dwell on all the face of the earth..." (*Acts* 17: 26).

Moroccan Bread
(Kisra or Khboz)

Makes 2 six-inch loaves

This is the caravan bread so typical of the Maghreb and North Africa in general. It is made with whole-wheat flour and oats which give it a characteristically rough texture. If you want a finer loaf, more like the Pita bread we are accustomed to in the West, use all-white flour. For centuries Moroccan families have made their loaves at home and sent them stamped with the family name to a communal bakery. There they are baked and returned home on the padded heads of children. The loaf rises only once and is formed into disks by hand, so it is very simple to make. In Marrakesh loaves are spiced with onion, cumin, parsley and paprika and then stuffed with butter or lard. The result is much like a savory scone, crisped like fry-bread from the inside out.

¼ cup warm water
1 package active dry yeast (2¼ teaspoons)
1 teaspoon sugar
1 cup whole wheat flour
3 ¼ cup unbleached white flour
½ cup old-fashioned rolled oats
   (not instant) or cracked barley
2 teaspoons salt
½ cup lukewarm whole milk
1 tablespoon aniseed, fennel seed,
   dill seed, caraway seed, poppy seed,
   nigella seed, or combination of these
1 tablespoon sesame seed
Cornmeal for dusting

28

In a small bowl stir to combine water, yeast and sugar. Allow to become bubbly and double in size. Meanwhile, in large bowl of standing electric mixer (or if kneading by hand use a large kitchen bowl and wooden spoon), use cookie paddle to pulse flours, oats and salt to combine.

Add the frothy yeast mixture and warm milk to the flour mixture. Add enough lukewarm water to make a stiff dough. The amount of water varies with humidity and flour, but I always start with one cup and add more as needed. Continue mixing on low with cookie paddle until mixture comes together to form a rough dough, then switch to the dough hook and knead on medium low for approximately 8-10 minutes. (If kneading by hand, turn out dough onto floured board and knead by pushing dough away from the body with the heel of the hand and then gather it back into a ball; repeat this motion. Hand kneading will take anywhere from 10-15 minutes.) During the last few minutes of kneading add the seeds. Form dough into two balls and allow to rest five minutes on the counter.

Lightly grease a large mixing bowl with olive oil. Coat a ball of dough with oil by swirling it around the inside of the bowl, making a cone shape as you do this. Transfer cone to a baking sheet sprinkled with cornmeal and flatten to a 5-inch round by pressing down on cone with palm of hand. Repeat with other ball of dough. Sprinkle each loaf with cornmeal and sesame seeds.

Cover baking sheet loosely with a damp towel and allow to rise in a warm, none-drafty place for 1 1/2 hours. (I preheat my oven to the lowest setting, then open the oven door for a minute to let the hot air out and then place the bread inside the closed oven to rise. This gives me a warm place which is undisturbed). Dough has risen properly if it does not spring back when poked with your finger.

Preheat oven to 400° F. Using a fork, prick the loaves around the outer edge and place in the middle of preheated oven. Bake 15 minutes, then lower heat to 300° and continue baking another 30 minutes. Bread is done when it sounds hollow when tapped on the bottom. Remove and allow to cool. Cut into wedges and serve with fresh butter and honey.

Très Hatch
Chef, Food Educator

From the book *Food for Foodies* used with permission of the author

*B*efore I became a bookseller, and more recently an editor, I might have written on friendship differently. But even then, as a reader, the idea that authors—and their characters—were more real to me, sources of solace, succor, entertainment, a lift, maybe even someone who might understand a knotty problem or share a celebration, or just provide an ear, drifted through my mind.

One book is often not enough to get the measure of a person—and every character within a tale carries a sliver at least of its creator in its genes; every idea or event has been conceived by that same intelligence—but if one reads an author's work as it is produced, or as one discovers it, there grows a sense of familiarity, of comfort, an idea that one has held long conversations with someone at just a bit of a distance. In short, the author has become a familiar, a

welcome voice. It may be an advantage that this friendship can be picked up or put down as one wishes.

But the distance is no more. Now I spend my days with authors in the flesh, and that immediacy shapes things differently, forces a closer examination of the basis of the interaction. It can be one so intense one almost shies away. Yet one is also drawn in; those I meet for the first time are eerily familiar, often in ways that surprise me. Certainly ways that go beyond the conversation at hand, ways that lay a deep background between us as if encountering a childhood friend one hasn't seen for years and delighting (or sorrowing, but mostly delighting) in them as an adult. And what I mostly find is that if I've liked the books, I like the person. It's virtually impossible to lie to readers; too much seeps out. And we, the author and I, come to share an intimacy, a closeness founded on the sorts of things you'd never up and say to a casual acquaintance, a well-met stranger. Some fairly fierce friendships have become mine with people I might see no more than once a year, if then. E-mail fosters this, making it possible not only to stay in touch but to share reciprocal thoughts, ideas, arguments, sensitivities, information—or just news. As my work load increases and my time to tend to ordinary friendships shrinks, I feel no sense of loss or loneliness, rather the circle of friends, and what they mean to me, gloriously expands.

One of the most crucial and defining moments of my life began when I was imprisoned shortly before the Soviet invasion of Afghanistan in 1979. During those long months in the torture-prison Sedarat, I shared a room with hundreds of men from all walks of life, each of us living under inhuman conditions. Some had been arrested because of their affiliation with the mujahidin; others were taken because they belonged to the opposition party.

There were countless other innocent ones, like the poor store owner who refused to sell eggs at a discount to a Communist Party member. It was several weeks before I learned that my own arrest had come about because my brother-in-law was involved in an attempted coup against the current regime. Prison officials hoped to gain information about him through me, and as a result, I was submitted to many weeks of torture.

In spite of our difficult circumstances, hope was something we tried to keep alive, no matter how faint the spark. And friendship was one of the things that kept that spark burning.

As inmates, we found consolation and strength in sharing our life's experiences and helping one another. I will never forget those men who kindly bathed my wounds after I had endured many hours of torture, even though they themselves were suffering.

Many of those inmates and friends have vanished into the abyss of time, but each one left me with an important message. There was the message of love from a young father to the baby he would never see because the arms of death were much closer to him than the tiny hands of his firstborn child. Then there was the message of a grandfather who eased our minds by telling us some of the wonderful fairy tales he once shared with his grandchildren. I will never forget the message of patriotism left by a silver-haired colonel who met death with a quiet smile. And always, I will carry with me the message of the single blood-red tear on my hand.

It happened one night around midnight when I heard soldiers bringing someone into the room next to ours. After the soldiers left, I heard the man moaning. It sounded like he was asking for water. Even though we weren't allowed to stand up in our room at night, I had to do something. I got a glass of water and started crawling on my elbows toward the next room. Inside, I found a young man lying on the cement floor. Even in the dim light, I could see that he was covered with blood. His face had so many cuts; all I could make out of his features were his big brown eyes.

Resting his head on my arm, I soaked one of the corners of my shirt in the glass of water and began wiping off the blood. He couldn't talk, but his lips were moving very slowly. I tried to give him a drink, but he was unable to swallow. I was trying to make him more comfortable when I saw one of his fingers move. Putting a hand under his head, I looked down into his face. With effort, the young man's eyes met mine.

A single tear came from the corner of one eye, slipped down the cuts on his face and hovered on his earlobe before dropping on my hand. By the time it reached my hand, that tear was as red as his blood. Then suddenly, he just stopped breathing.

I couldn't believe this was happening. I was only twenty-two and this was the first time someone had died in my arms. Leaning over, I kissed his forehead; then I closed his eyes. Tears ran down my cheeks and fell on his young face, which I cleaned for the last time.

I got to my feet without fear of being seen or shot and returned to my room. No one asked any questions because the answer was already written on my face.

Sleep did not come that night. For some reason, that last look and that tear changed me. There hadn't been a word between us—only a glance and a single tear—yet somehow, I could feel his deepest emotions. I understood his pain and his sorrow. I knew how much he wanted to have another human being next to him during the last moments of his life. I have no idea whether he saw me as a member of his family, a friend, or an angel, but during that brief time, I truly felt like his closest friend and brother.

This man left me with the sad, but profound reminder that no matter how different we seem to be, we are all alike once we remove the thick curtain that blinds our truer, deeper vision of one another.

The bonds of friendship are stronger than any prison walls. Over twenty years have passed since I left Sedarat, yet in my mind, I can still see the faces of the friends I knew there. Because of them, the old Afghan saying has even deeper meaning for me: "Pain shared is half pain; happiness shared is double."

From the book *A Square Sky* by Sayed Ahmad Sharifi
Published by Granite Publishing
Used with permission of the author

It has been said that you probably will be able to count on one hand the number of "true friends" that you will have in your lifetime; many acquaintances, few true friends.

A true friend is a priceless gift; someone in whom you can have absolute trust and confidence. Someone with whom you can share your innermost thoughts, worries, weaknesses, concerns, dreams, ambitions, your "life" without fear and criticism or rejection, knowing that your friend truly cares for you and would never betray you for any reason.

A true friend asks nothing and gives everything, always asking "What can I do to make you happy?" Acquaintances ask "What can you do to make me happy? What is in it for me?"

A true friend accepts you for what you are and at the same time honestly tries to help you to become the very best you can and want to be.

A true friend glories in your achievements and recognition for what you do and is never jealous.

One of the greatest pains you will ever experience is when a person you considered your true friend betrays you.

Unfortunately, most people go through life never having the joy to be realized from having and being a true friend. To have a true friend requires that you be a true friend; one of the most noble of all life's goals.

35

ELAINE HUBER
OFFICE MANAGER

conducted a survey among my co-workers. They all said that to them, friendship meant trust. A friend was someone you could confide in and they would not judge you.

A long time ago I was having some very stressful marital problems. I confided in my best friend and neighbor. She came to me several days later and asked if I would mind if she told her husband what I had said. I could not believe that she had held our conversation in such confidence that she would not even tell her spouse. I knew then that I could trust that friend with anything.

A friend is someone who will be there for you in good times or bad. She will laugh with you and cry with you. She will support you in all you do.

And what is a friend? More than a father, more than a brother: a traveling companion, with him, you can conquer the impossible, even if you must lose it later. Friendship marks a life even more deeply than love. Love risks degenerating into obsession, friendship is never anything but sharing. It is to a friend that you communicate the awakening of desire, the birth of the vision or a terror, the anguish of seeing the sun disappear or of finding that order and justice are no more. That's what you can talk about with a friend. Is the soul immortal, and if so why are we afraid to die? If God exists, how can we lay claim to freedom, since He is its beginning and its end? What is death, when you come down to it? The closing of a parenthesis, and nothing more? And what about life? In the mouth of a philosopher, these questions may have a false ring, but asked during adolescence or friendship, they have the power to change being: a look burns and ordinary gestures tend to transcend themselves. What is a friend? Someone who for the first time makes you aware of your loneliness and his, and helps you to escape so you in turn can help him. Thanks to him you can hold your tongue without shame and talk freely without risks. That's it.

From *Gates of the Forest* by Elie Wiesel pages 26-27
Used with permission of the author.

I have a friend, her name is Kailyn. She's been my friend ever since I was two and she was four years of age. It's really special to have a friend for nine years even through the toughest moments. We're still really good friends even though she's older than me. It seems like she is my age. If somebody makes fun of me she'll tell them to stop. If friends are yucky they're not real friends. To me friendship is what I have with Kailyn. We never let each other down. If I was sad she would cheer me up, if she was sad I would cheer her up. I'm really glad she is my friend. I hope she always will be.

It is Sunday afternoon in New York. I am relaxing in my house in Queens, ready to start a new week of work tomorrow. I'm sitting in front of my computer, thinking about friendship… it is raining outside…

I will be thirty-seven years in a few months, and I had many people I used to call friends throughout my entire life. It is somehow sad to say I do not have any contact with the majority of them anymore. Were they real friends? Or were they only general acquaintances? I do not know. However, each one of them reflects a moment of my life and a moment of growth of my personality, my character and the human being I am today.

A few of them though, are still with me today, and I still share with them my daily experiences, my questions about who I am, my quest for answers and my need of support and advice.

I left Italy in 1999 to move to New York and I abandoned everything I had there to start a new adventure, to face a new challenge, to make it happen. I was 33. Together with all the rest, I left behind three young women I used to spend all my time with in Milan; my best friends Giulia, Mariapaola and Ruth.

We used to go places together, see people together, drive around town, go to clubs, go out, laugh about everything and everybody, go shopping, or just visit and talk for hours about our experiences, our life, our jobs, all our troubles and tribulations…

I had the greatest time of my life with these women, and I still miss them a lot. However, I never left them for real and I still share with them everything. Giulia is now pregnant, and I am already planning the possibility to be in Milan at the end of

39

the year when she will have her baby (I am right now "the American aunt"). Mariapaola and Ruth are single, always challenged by the need of independence and the natural need to be in a relationship with the right man at the right time. I still talk to them at least every two weeks on the phone, and thanks to Internet and messenger, I chat with them every day. I still share with them my life and my daily tribulations. I still love them as much as possible. And I visit every year and spend some time with them to catch up, give my advice, get their advice and hug them as much as I can! No matter where I am and no matter how far away, I know I'm in their heart as much as they are in mine. And I'm sure there is no better friendship than this; a feeling deep enough to ignore time and distance, past and present; presence and absence.

Mariapaola, who I chat with everyday through messenger, is just so important for me. My day is not the same if I don't have the possibility to know that she's okay, how her day is going, how are the other two girls doing, what is going on in Milan and all the possible things two women can share, openly and happily.

I moved to New York to be with Damone; the man that today is my husband and the one who is now my best friend.

He makes me want to be a better person everyday, in every occasion, during every new challenge. He helps me succeed, get better, and he's always by my side, making me the best I can be, always. No competition, no envy, no antagonism; a real support out of love.

These are the people I call friends, today. I think friendship does not get much better than that.

Friendship to me is always having a good friend to hang out with, to build memories with, and to help make you who you are. A true close friend is someone who will always be there for you in any situation, to listen to any problems you have and help you through those problems, to help you make the right decisions, or just listening and being supportive. A true friend is also someone you can share the best of times with and be happy with when things in life are going great.

They should compliment you on your success in life and also on the small, less meaningful things in life. That is a true friend to me. Although I have not experienced this with a friend, I am very happy and thankful to say I have this kind of friendship with my mother.

41

There are many friends in my heart's garden, flowers of friendship which decorate my life with their color and beauty, turning this sometimes barren plot of living into a refuge and a haven. They are quite varied, these friendly flowers of mine.

Some blossomed slowly over time, others in an instant of recognition. Some budding relationships required hours of care to cultivate and maintain—and at times seemed hardly worth the trouble— while others thrived with the barest hint of attention. Some seem more exotic showpieces than friends, and though surrounded by others in the garden, they remain solitary. Some of my most endearing friends, like wildflowers, may seem too common to notice, yet they are the hardiest of all, withstanding cold frosts of conflict, plagues of gossiping locusts, and droughts of disinterest. And there are yet one or two flowers which grow in the secret walled corners of my heart, hidden by shade and mossy with memory. But of all my flowering friends, three sweet blossoms are uniquely dear. They are treasured not only because they are truly mine—planted, grown and cared for—but because my three children are my very dearest friends.

My first and eldest flower is a tulip: bright, red, and simply appealing. He returns after winter snows, tall and confident in the spring sunshine, an instant comfort and companion. Clouds travel past, shadow and sun blow by, but this flower is unwavering. His heart is open for all to see: kind, true, and unflinching. Cold days are warmer with him, and heat less oppressive. His direct understanding of life—its beginnings and endings—are like himself, vibrant in the spring, waiting in the winter.

My second flower is a rose; a poem, perfumed and perfect. She is the many petaled dance in the breeze, the thorn of whit and intellect, the fairy's heart unfolding. In her smile is an endless sunset; grace and elegance without effort. She is sweetly unaware of her own ability to enchant, yet her spells are cast nonetheless, and all around her laugh and sing just from growing near her. This heavenly hybrid far exceeds the plant from which she has sprung, yet when gazed upon, my childhood returns, fairy tales are true, and all dreams are trembling with truth and realization.

My third and final flower is a tiger lily— bold and adventurous, and indomitable. He is spectacular and yet subtle, perennial in humor, annual in temperament. He adores without reservation, throwing down roots with absolute confidence in his right to be there. This flower, like his name, has dual attributes. He is both brave and tender, wild, yet vulnerably affectionate. He will defend all around him, choke weeds without hesitation, then lazily bask in the hot summer sun. He believes all the garden is his: to amuse, to protect, and to love.

Of all the friends in my heart's garden these three grow best. With my children twined about my heart, I will never lie fallow, cold cannot remain, and no distressful amount of weeds can make me feel unkempt. All other friendships could fade and fail, yet these three: my tulip, my rose, and my tiger lily, are all any gardener could hope for and more than I ever dreamed.

I encounter many people in my daily routine connecting library users with information they request. Some transactions are short and sweet while others may require great detail. Some even result in friendship.

Just the other day after a library transaction with a patron, she expressed interest in my thoughts about the meaning of friendship. Immediately, three childhood friends came to mind. The bonds of love we have experienced over the years have strengthened over time. We enjoy sharing the news of our families and delight in updates of our recent adventures. We respect and honor the lifelong connections we've shared. Like gold, friendships are refined by our life experiences.

We talked about different types of friendship and how they enrich our lives. I remembered a precious life changing experience: in 1974 I met two women from our church community. We were to become true friends. They brought a unique handcrafted quilt to our beautiful new baby Joshua. It was turquoise and white gingham checks with teddy bears. It became Joshua's favorite blanket. From the first moment everything about Joshua was special. He was born with Treacher Collins Syndrome. His facial features were underdeveloped, requiring us to feed him by the Gavage Method, inserting a feeding tube through his nose and into his stomach. It was a challenging experience. When Joshua was 18 months old, he was ready for reconstructive surgery that would correct his "soft" palate, create a roof in his mouth and allow him to begin to eat normally.

Unfortunately, they were complications even after the surgery. With Joshua's short

44

jaw some foods were difficult to swallow. He aspirated a morsel of bread blocking his airway. Joshua lost consciousness. Now in a coma, Joshua had his family, many prayers, and the special blanket to protect him. After four days he began showing marked signs of improvement only to regress when he discovered his blanket was missing. It had been permanently lost in the hospital laundry.

My husband and I felt compelled to attend mass the following morning. We needed assurance and hope. Although Joshua was out of the coma he was depressed and the news had already reached our small church community. With concern, the ladies who had given us the blanket asked about him. I was so filled with sadness and worry I could not answer their questions. It was my husband who told the story of the missing blanket. The women were kind and promised to offer prayers for Joshua.

At the ICU (Intensive Care Unit) we found little Joshua in his crib huddled under the hospital blankets, which were white like everything else. We comforted him the best we could. Later that afternoon when a nurse came into the room holding a special delivery, we saw Joshua's face light up. She had a new quilt identical to his lost favorite, turquoise and white gingham checks with teddy bears. My two friends had lovingly made another quilt that very day. It had taken them seven hours.

Their generous gesture lingers in my memory today. To me friendship is love given freely, with no strings attached, a healing and life-giving gift, and like gold, refined over time.

45

Growing up I was always told that everybody in the world is your friend. Now that I'm older, I've come to realize that a friend is somebody who listens and understands, somebody you can always depend on, somebody that's nice and cares about you. I've also come to appreciate my best friend, because I know she is that kind of person.

One of my favorite quotes is, "Once in a while, you'll find a friend who will be your friend forever." I like this quote because I think that it is very realistic. A true friend is hard to find. I think a true friend is somebody you would die for, somebody that means the world to you, that if you split, you would always find each other again.

I think friends are extremely important because they help you get through a lot of stressful events. They are people you can turn to for advice and who would never cheat you. A friend is someone who would stand by your side in good times and bad, someone who does anything to brighten your day, who believes in you.

A friend is someone you can laugh with, even if the thing you are laughing at isn't funny at all. A friend is someone you can trust, like a diary, putting all your secret thoughts inside, someone you've shared a lot with, someone who respects you and is respected back. A friend is like a key, a key to unlock all your happiness. One can also compare friends to a good book, sometimes they make you laugh, and at other times, they comfort you. There are good books, and there are bad books, but the best books are kept with you forever.

46

The history of the country now called the Republic of Georgia goes back to the 5th century B.C. Customs, traditions, and the lifestyle of the country are based on friendship and that's why friendship in Georgia is considered to be the most valuable phenomenon. Here, friends are like members of one's family. Parents teach their children how to make friends and maintain their friendship for the remainder of their lives. I have many friends, some of them since my childhood, some since college, and some of them are my co-workers. But all of them are very important to me, and I can not imagine my life without them.

To be a friend means to take obligations and responsibilities, have the ultimate trust, and share all your happiness and grief. In Georgia one depends on friends as much as on one's family, and in times of distress they are there to support you unconditionally and without any questions. Friends are always glad to be with you, extending their kindness and happiness.

47

An acquaintance begins when you meet someone. You become that person's friend when you do something for him or her, when you become involved and get to know them. Sometimes I hesitate because I'm afraid I might not do it well, but when I've gone ahead, I've never been sorry.

48

At the beginning of my life in America, I became infused with the belief that in this country nothing was impossible, and I was always involved in different projects. Not all of them were successful. To make me feel better and to justify the occasional defeat, people would tell me "Well, you can't make a silk purse out of a sow's ear."

The expression was often accompanied by a sigh. I didn't adopt such an attitude and felt delightfully vindicated when I saw an elegant silk purse made from a pig's ear in a glass case at the Smithsonian in Washington, D.C.. An American scientist had accomplished the seemingly impossible some time in the 1920s. Through dedicated research he had found that components of a pig's ear have similarities with those of silk.

It was all I needed. From then on I responded to any "no" as a "yes" on a detour.

Unless there was clear evidence that it would hurt anyone, immediately or later, I went ahead with the task at hand.

I met my match in the late 1980s while working in the Soviet Union. One day, my doctor friend Mamuka called to let me know that he had to visit a patient in Svaneti, a mountainous, isolated region of Georgia, USSR. I immediately accepted his invitation for my interpreter and me to fly with him to this often inaccessible area. Throughout the year the seasons determine admission by either helicopter or car. As far as I knew, only a few of my Georgian friends had made that journey.

How could I say no to such an opportunity? The rugged beauty of Svaneti had appealed to the romantic side of my nature ever since I first heard about it through folklore and legend. The

49

inhabitants, famous for their independence, are known as the Swans, one of the original ethnic groups of the country. Anciently they lived there in tall, crenelated stone towers, some of which are between eight hundred to twelve hundred years old. The towers were built as refuge against the harsh elements and perhaps even more importantly, for safety during attacks by unfriendly forces. A number of these imposing structures—protected by the government for their historical and architectural value—still survive, but until now I had only seen them in photographs.

Takeoff in Helicopter #22756 was scheduled for 12:30 p.m. We arrived at the airport well within the typical Georgian time frame, which meant that we were one hour late, but no one seemed unduly concerned.

I was worried about a different matter.

In the excitement of the moment, I had overlooked an important detail, permission from O.V.I.R., the Department of Visas and Registration, to leave the city. Everywhere in the Soviet Union, foreigners had to register within two days of their arrival, and again when they needed to travel for any distance.

The process could take some time. Assured of a captive audience, an official had once given me an in-depth Georgian history lesson. By now the authorities recognized me, they had become less strict, but this was, after all the USSR and foreigners were not allowed just to hop on a plane and fly around the countryside. Regrettably, Mamuka only noticed my oversight after we arrived at the airport. There was little we could do now.

I had often been told that if Soviet citizens waited for everything to move through official, bureaucratic channels little would get accomplished. As a result, people found creative and sometimes unorthodox solutions to their problems. But on this occasion my friends outdid themselves. Effortlessly, they carried the practice a whole step further. Given the time constraints, and to justify my presence on the Svaneti trip, they invented a new identity for me. On paper, I would be Dr. Doris Stromberg, Neurosurgeon from Latvia.

To my way of thinking, the idea had a number of serious flaws; the most obvious being that I did not have any medical training. Such a misrepresentation could easily land me in jail, and a Soviet jail at that. The fact that I did not speak or understand one word of Latvian seemed minor by comparison. Even more importantly, was it worth it for my friends to take such a risk just so I could have this opportunity? This was a level of

friendship I had never experienced; it was definitely not what I had in mind when I voiced the wish to go to Svaneti some day.

My concerns did not hinder the plan from moving ahead. I was instructed to stay in the airport terminal while my friends took care of the "necessary arrangements." I sensed no nervousness on their part. On the contrary, they seemed to thrive on this kind of situation. To them it was a challenge. I warmed to it more gradually. The plot was serious enough for me to voice some misgivings.

"What happens if it doesn't work?" I dared ask when they returned.

"Then we go to plan B."

"And what is plan B?"

"We don't know yet. Let's see if plan A works. Leave everything to us and don't speak until we're on board." Common sense and conscience told me I was doing something very stupid, but I managed to ignore both. To my relief, we never had to put plan B to the test because no one checked my papers.

Our helicopter was much larger than I expected. It had five portholes on each side of its approximately twelve meter long frame. A few collapsible benches served as seats. There was no padding and no armrests in this stripped down model. Function, not comfort, had been the main ingredient in its construction.

This Soviet workhorse of the skies finds its greatest use in taking supplies to mountain villages, and being of assistance during avalanches or special cases like our errand today. If needed, it could seat twenty-two passengers. On this trip there were eight. Five of the passengers on board were the sons of Mamuka's patient. They had come to him to seek medical help for their mother.

During the first part of our trip, visibility was limited. It was odd to observe clouds outside the chopper's windows and through gaps in the not too tightly fitting metal sections between my feet. Eventually, the clouds thinned and gave way. There was little noticeable sign of habitation. Once in a while, I had glimpses of cattle running in energetic spurts, trying to flee from the helicopter's shadow. Viewed from above, much of the region looked like a lush green carpet although it was late summer. Here and there, strips of golden corn, rusty metal roofs and winding, ochre-colored roads could be seen. Then the valleys closed up again, and forested mountains took over.

When the helicopter reached an altitude of 2000 meters, patches of snow became more numerous. Among Svaneti's many dagger-like peaks, ten are taller than Mont Blanc in the European Alps. Some mountains seemed near enough to touch as we threaded our way through the narrow passages. It was not always safe for even a helicopter to venture into this forbidding territory, but today the comforting click of cockpit instruments told me all was well.

Two hours after take-off, we landed in the middle of a boulder-strewn cow pasture. A waiting jeep took us up a steep, potholed dirt road. The gravity of Mamuka's patient's illness was confirmed by the number of relatives and friends present at the house when we arrived. We were welcomed by the husband of the critically ill woman. He was a compactly-built man, with a deeply lined, wind burned face and hands that knew how to mend things. Concern for his lifetime companion showed in his eyes. Both husband and wife were in their mid-eighties. They had grown up in the same village, married and had seven children. Now his wife was suffering from heart problems, sclerosis, and complications from diabetes which had resulted in gangrene.

The latter condition might require the amputation of a leg. Mamuka had been summoned to save her from that fate, because the woman wanted to die with her body intact, but the prognosis did not offer much hope. While Mamuka examined his patient, my interpreter and I discreetly left and walked around the property. It was obvious that this family prided itself on being self-sufficient. Here, people live close to the seasons and what they can coax from the earth. Through necessity and will much is grown or produced by them on their own

53

land. A few cows, a large pig, some goats and chickens shared a pasture. There was also a garden with rows of herbs, potatoes, beans and other vegetables, but the need for beauty had not been neglected. In a corner of the yard, space had been made for a flower bed.

For safety reasons, family members do most of their cooking in a one room kitchen house a short distance from the main dwelling. Standing in the open doorway I could feel waves of heat coming from the wood-burning stove. I watched the choreography of people accustomed to working together. One woman was stirring something aromatic

in a large black kettle; another was kneading dough on a wooden board. As soon as she not-iced my interest, she kindly took the time to share her bread-making technique.

Though one of their own was faced with a serious medical situation, family members and neighbors had prepared a big dinner for us. It was a welcome in its most elemental and ancient form, without uncertainty over priorities or values. To them, hospitality, the breaking of bread, is a sacrament, symbolic of emotional and mental nourishment; neglecting any detail was unthinkable even now.

When we washed our hands at an outside spigot, one woman shyly handed us a bar of soap, another one stood by with a rough-spun cotton towel. Afterwards we were directed up three flights of narrow wooden stairs to a formal parlor. Like so many other Georgian meals I had eaten, the one awaiting us was rich in variety.

Tomato and cucumber salads, and salads made from beets; then there was a pizza topped with cheese, another one was filled with a bean paste and seasoned with herbs and spices; next came fried and boiled potatoes; and chicken, mutton and beef; some grilled, some broiled, some fried; hot, and cold eggplant dishes, sprinkled with deep red pomegranate seeds; aromatic bread fresh from the oven, red and white wine, water and lemonade to drink; grapes, pears and apples, and cakes and cookies for dessert.

Our pilot, copilot and navigator were both friends and honored guests. They sat facing the open door, to keep a close eye on weather conditions. People appreciate these daring men, who often risk their lives to help others. The patient's husband was no exception. He graciously offered the first toast to the "Knights of the sky, who challenge the mountains."

Though we were invited to stay, our pilot grew increasingly concerned about dark billowing clouds moving in our direction. We drove pell-mell down the mountain; some free-roaming pigs ran squealing out of the way. Take-off came none too soon, as a storm rapidly descended. Close by, thunderheads rumbled a warning, but we would not return home just yet. Because of the long periods between these infrequent flights much has to be accomplished.

Our helicopter dipped and swooped like a swallow, dropping off parcels and picking up passengers in places invisible to me until we were right above them. And when a friend or neighbor asked a favor of the crew, another unscheduled stop was made. Response to someone's needs came at a moments notice, without much discussion.

We never did meet Mamuka's patient. From the beginning he had feared that she was beyond help and that is how it turned out to be. He had reached the limit of what his words and his skill could do for her. Those who loved her knew it with a sad certainty, yet they would carry on because their circumstances did not allow for self-pity or delusions.

I had wanted to travel to Svaneti because of its scenery. Pictures do not do justice to this harsh, beautiful land, but the real riches are the people. They have much of what ultimately matters; their relationships so clean and untarnished that to an outsider the experience felt like stepping on Holy Ground. I had been allowed more of an entry than was due a stranger and would never forget this soul-enriching passage.

"Dr. Stromberg" and her companions arrived safely back in the city as dusk approached. The day had been much like a long drink from the well.

DSP

The quality of friendship you give reflects
the quality of person you are.

*O*love my work. I can't put it into words, I love it that much. The best days are walking the fields with the wild birds singing, especially the larks. I'm out in all weathers, particularly during lambing time.

I'm happy in my own company. I'm never lonely and I'm never bored. But I like talking to people too, and when I'm traveling I seem to meet other shepherds and farmers and fall into conversation. It has happened to me in the Highlands where I live, but also in Australia, New Zealand and Hawaii.

One day I was driving on a long, deserted road in Scotland and passed a wee house. I'd often had a word with the old man who lived there, and this time when I stopped he asked me to have tea with him. We fell to talking, and I discovered that we were related. He was eighty-two then, and partly disabled.

He told me he was planning a trip to Australia to visit family, and asked me if I would travel with him and look after him. I was going to New Zealand myself, so I said I would.

It was a wonderful journey, and the flight crew looked after us rather too well. Every time they brought the rest of us tea, they gave him a very large dram of whiskey without water. By the time we neared landing at Perth he was out cold. The poor stewardess was frightened because he was ill, then was awfully embarrassed when she knew the truth. We had to get a wheelchair to take my friend off. And there was I who came to look after him, and didn't even know his family except from a photograph.

I searched every face in the waiting mass of people and eventually found a beard that looked like the one in the photo and made straight for him. He had with him a woman a few years older than me. They were horrified when they saw the old man in the chair, until I explained that he was only drunk, and that it was not really his fault. For a moment there was silence; then the woman burst out laughing. From that time Elma and I were friends.

The old man was a bit less than good tempered, and a bit of a handful. We backed each other up in looking after him. I never went on to New Zealand. I stayed with them the whole three months and never felt more welcome or at ease. We got to know each other so comfortably I could start a sentence and she would finish it. Neither she nor I had a sister by blood, but we found one in that time. We had a ball.

To me that is friendship, natural, easy, interesting, with plenty to talk about. There is honesty in friendship, and never condescension. You can talk openly and gain trust. I don't dwell on the past. I think positive and look forward. But I like to reminisce about the good things that happened, with the people who shared them with me. Elma and I write and visit when we can. Friendship is what makes life so enjoyable, and if you don't try, if you don't go there, you'll never know.

JOIE BATCHELOR
NINETY-TWO YEAR OLD RETIREE

A friend is a communicator who listens.

$\mathscr{I}$ feel honored to be asked to share some personal thoughts on the subject of friendship. The subject is very relevant for our times when religious extremism, nationalism, and terrorism are destroying the very foundations of human civilization. It is my deep conviction that true friendship is possible—through faith in Jesus Christ who taught us to love each other and be a friend to the needy.

61

The things in my life that have meaning and truth have all come from friendships shared between people I have met and grown to know. Sometimes only for a fleeting second in their lives, I have had an opportunity to help, whatever the need. It would have taken so much longer to know what I was here to do if I didn't have these friends, my family, my career, and the BRT (big red truck).

Sometimes instant help is needed by a small child that can't wake her mother; the cry from a mother who recognizes the crumpled, broken bicycle in the middle of the street and needs to know if her daughter is going to be okay. Seeing a small child leave in a helicopter isn't a comforting feeling, but my job is to comfort the mother also, as though I were her best friend. Or the father that was building a playhouse for his children, when he fell from the roof and now can't feel his legs. It is to see the look on the face of the son as his mother passes away. Or the middle aged man recognizing that his chest pain is more than just the pizza he had for lunch.

At times I didn't even know that it was a comfort to see and hear us as we were arriving to the scene of an emergency. I observe and participate in these things close up because of my occupation, the lights and siren on the BRT announce that help is here and we are your friends. This is only one type of friendship we experience. Often it sneaks up on us by disguising itself in a form that we would not recognize so easily. It is the FDNY (Fire Department, New York) firefighter we met at ground zero who had not left the pile for seven days, looking for his friends whether or not they had ever met.

As we move through life, we try to

recognize the little steps other people take to make friends. I never dreamt that in nineteen-ninety-six, I would be asked to go to Tbilisi, Georgia to teach our techniques to firefighters over there, or that on September 18, 2001, I would be deployed to New York City with our urban research and rescue team. The paths we take and the trails we make leave impressions in the minds of all people we come in contact with. Let them be those of friendship and love.

hen asked to write a few notes on what friendship means to me I find myself reflecting most on the friendships I have now and the friendships I seek to have. I decided to make a list of words that I feel describe the gifts of friendship. They are as follows…

Happiness Courage Honor

Trust Sympathy Kindness

Healing Strength Knowledge

Forgiveness Caring Open-minded

Laughter Loyalty Understanding

Guiding Patient Love

Safe Life Devotion

Honest Joy Meaning

After creating this list I also find myself looking at the meaning of each of these words. I came to the realization that I meet or hear about people everyday that exemplify at least one of the words I used to describe them. In a world that is constantly changing I feel we should all take the time to make a list that would describe our ideal friendship.

It was the summer of 1969, the summer of Woodstock, a summer that will be remembered for the variety of historic events that took place. One of them being that NASA was in the process of putting a manned flight on the moon. These would be the first known human steps on that arid surface! It was an incredible moment in the history of man; a moment that stretched the mind and the imagination. All over the world radio and television were covering the historic event. Millions of eyes and ears were focused on the actions of the heroic astronauts aboard Apollo 11. The advanced technology involved to accomplish such a feat was well beyond the grasp of most and imagined by only a few. This event united not only a nation, but for a brief time, the entire world.

At that very moment, on a back road on the island of Maui, I was involved in what seemed to me an equally astounding, if not internationally intriguing, feat. A 1950 Chevy that three friends and I had "borrowed" to circumference the island was well stuck in the sand along a beautiful stretch of beach. Thinking that nothing could stop the forward momentum of four adventurous lads, we had directed the car into the sand, hoping to reach the stretch of road on the other side.

This particular summer we had come to work for the Maui Pineapple Company. Nine hours a day, six days a week, we stalked the unsuspecting pineapple, shoulder to shoulder, eleven across. Down the rows of prickly plants we marched in search of the ripening fruit. Filling the truck to its ten-ton capacity, it would then carry the pineapple back to the cannery, where the fruit would

65

be juiced and shipped stateside.

The summer of 1969 spent on the island of Maui cemented a bond with four friends that continues to this day. We had all met in junior high and high school and had become an inseparable group. Our summer in Hawaii was only one chapter in a lifelong friendship that has endured disagreements, comings and goings, not seeing each other for years on end and any other obstacle that the world can throw into the path of friendship. Many evenings have been passed since that summer in re-hashing the stories from our "pine-picking" days and other adventures. Credit our wives for smiling and laughing at tales they must have heard a hundred times as if they were hearing them for the first time.

That friendship is as fresh, deep and honest today as it was when we were sixteen.

We shared every type of personal experience friends can share: musical performances, road journeys, deep conversations late into the night, illnesses, broken hearts, weddings, divorces, children, and our individual searches for personal improvement. I must know the other four as well as I do anyone. Those friendships are very dear to me and I can imagine forty years from now sitting on a front porch somewhere, talking and listening to the crickets as Dux recalls some small detail from our "venture around the island" that will surely bring a smile to the lips of Matt, Jim, Big Jim and myself.

With true friendship there is often a feeling of knowing what another needs and wants without it being spoken. I have had such experiences with those I am very close to and found that if this feeling is not invalidated, there can be a deepening of the relationship. I have also found that if I truly care for someone, I am willing to try to see his or her side of things even if I disagree. In fact, more importantly, especially if I disagree. To allow another to share his or her thoughts and viewpoints, without criticizing or interrupting, can go a long way to creating a closer bond. The value I place on friendship demands that I take the time and show the patience necessary to allow another to have his or her say, while I listen with an open heart. There are many rare jewels in this world, but true friendship is the rarest of all. Keep it safe, polish it and it will shine brighter than any gem.

I had been a fan of Gary Cooper's since I was ten years old. The thought of acting with him was a little staggering. He became a star with his first feature film at the end of the silent era and became even more prominent with the coming of sound. He was, and remained till his death, a movie star when that meant a lot more than it does now—principally, that your name on a marquee more or less guaranteed a success.

There's a great deal to be said about Coop. For one thing, he was a far better actor than he was given credit for, with a deft comic touch and an understated impact in serious roles. Within his range (defined in part by his size and formidable presence), he was a riveting actor. When young, he'd been incredibly handsome, with a face born for the camera; as he aged, that face became a map of America. Indeed, along with Jimmy Stewart and Hank Fonda, he was an iconic image of the American male. If this wasn't what the American man was, it was what he was supposed to be.

On screen, you couldn't take your eyes off Coop; he listened as well as any actor I've worked with. Looking at daily footage every evening, when I was supposed to be checking out my own performance, I found myself watching him instead. (Any film actor will tell you that is most unusual.)

The film "Wreck of the Mary Deare" was scheduled to wrap shooting with two weeks in London, mostly exteriors. For such a short location time, my wife Lydia stayed home, as did Coop's wife, Rocky. We found ourselves camping out in neighboring bachelor suites at the Savoy.

Making a film, or a play, forces a fierce, focused intimacy on everyone involved. You all need each other healthy and stable to get it down, like a combat air crew, or an infantry platoon. They are often men and women you've never met before, but you are all married to each other till the shoot is finished or the play closes. After that, you often hardly keep in touch, until the next time.

I don't make friends easily; those closest to me are mostly people I've known for decades. Gary Cooper was twenty-some years older than I; he must have looked on me as a young stud actor coming up. In addition, he was a rather shy man, as I am myself. Still, unlikely as it seems, we became friends.

Like film, with its images of light and shadow, very often friendship speaks most eloquently without superficial dialogue. We didn't talk much about acting. In school, you talk about nothing else — passionate acolytes searching for the Holy Grail. Once it becomes your life, that search is usually internal and private.

Coop was marvelously funny. He handled situations with a cool ease that amazed me. One evening we'd had dinner at an excellent steakhouse off Berkeley Square. Leaving, we passed a table of young mods and rockers, the London equivalent of today's punk rock kids, with special wardrobe and haircuts. As Coop walked by, one of them said, "Oh, there goes the big cowboy star."

Coop stopped, turned in his tracks, and looked steadily at the young man. "When you say that, smile," he said softly. The kid couldn't have realized that was a line from Cooper's first hit film, "The Virginian," but it didn't matter. Suddenly, he wasn't in a cozy London restaurant anymore, but standing all alone on a dusty western street, with a chill wind at the back of his neck. No one at

69

the table moved or looked up. Coop stood there for fully thirty seconds, cold-eyed, then smiled lightly, turned on his heel, and walked out. As I joined him in the back of his Rolls, I said, "You read that line very well, Coop."

He grinned and straightened the crease in his Savile Row trousers. "Well," he said, "I've had lots of practice."

I don't know another actor who'd have dared even try that, let alone make it stick.

From *In the Arena* by Charlton Heston
Simon & Schuster, 1995
Used with permission of the Author

70

have long believed that no one gets up in the morning with the intention of causing unhappiness to others. This philosophy has served me well wherever life has taken me, from driving on freeways to navigating relationships.

But once in a while I have needed a reminder. I had that opportunity when a plane's mechanical problem delayed my transatlantic flight. Most passengers adapted to the temporary inconvenience with good grace. Not so for a slender, aristocratic-looking woman in her late seventies. She appeared to take the announcement as a personal affront and responded accordingly.

Sitting some distance away in the airport lounge, I watched airline personnel fill her increasingly irritated demands for refreshments, reading material, and updated flight information.

The delay lasted three hours. I pity the person sitting next to her, I thought, observing the woman among the first to board.

As luck would have it, I was that person. Our ten-hour flight loomed agonizingly long. My imperious fellow traveler soon told me that she had never been able to sleep in the daylight and definitely not on a plane. I acknowledged her comment with a weary nod, so tired I could have fallen asleep anywhere.

She continued to engage me in conversation until it seemed the only polite way to escape was to excuse myself and close my eyes.

Her sudden, sharp intake of breath startled me from a brief rest. When I asked if she was hurting, she answered with a brusque, "It's bearable."

Only then did I notice the etchings of

71

pain on her face. At that instant two sayings came to my mind: the first, a line from a favorite hymn, "Who am I to judge another When I walk imperfectly?" And the second, an old Portuguese adage, "Slowly, we go far."

Obviously, I had yet far to go. Ashamed of my earlier unwillingness, I made a much-needed mental adjustment and changed course. If ten hours of my time would help this woman, then surely I could give them to her.

Talking seemed to have a calming effect on my traveling companion. She was well informed on the politics and the geography of countries many people might have difficulty finding on a map. Her expertise on a wide variety of subjects amazed me. Her sharing of personal experiences enriched me. Slowly, the woman's story unfolded.

A native of Greece, she had been secretary to the queen of that country in her youth. When she fell in love with an officer of the German occupational forces during World War II, her family sent her away in disgrace, first to England and then to America. There, she eventually married. Unable to have children, she chose to devote her life to community service.

She had been widowed some months when she learned that she had an incurable disease. Now she was returning from a trip to her homeland, where she had said goodbye to the remaining members of her family.

When we said our own good-byes, I knew that I had taken a most enriching journey with someone both demanding and compassionate. Two weeks later, a card arrived in the mail. It read in part:

"My Dearest Friend! It was the best trip for me to be with you all that time. God sent you to sit next to me and take the pain away. For those hours I did not feel it."

We stayed in touch for almost a year, until one day her letters stopped. Her name was Maria, and I miss her still.

DSP

About twenty years ago a friend of mine, her four teenage children and I took a driving holiday around Britain. We talked about all manner of things, ideas, experiences and feelings. My friend did not meet my parents, but I told her how my mother had been born on the coast of Northumberland, and had always loved the sea. As a tiny child she had played on the beach at Dunstanborough and heard stories of the ruins of the castle half buried by the sea. She had fallen in love with the sea and had simply walked into it, glorying in its beauty and power, until rescued by her frantic mother.

Even as an adult she visited the coast again and again, but time and fortune had taken her inland. She now lived in a city, and did not expect to realize her dream of returning to the coast.

My friend resolved immediately to take something from Dunstanborough Beach and its magic back to my mother. She would collect shells of different kinds, smooth pebbles and some seaweed, both red and green, and enough seawater to keep them fresh. But what could she put them in? A bottle! Something my mother could keep and enjoy.

We did not have such a thing, so we stopped the car outside a rough cottage by the shore, with an untidy garden and crooked gates. My friend walked up the path and knocked at a paint-peeled door. After a moment or two it was opened by a middle-aged man with a cigarette hanging from the corner of his lip, and a beer can in his hand.

My friend asked if he had a bottle he could give her. He said of course he had, and asked why she wanted it. She told him it was to take a memory of the sea to a lady who loved it and might not come to it again.

"Ah!" He said. "In that case just any bottle won't do, it has to be something special." He disappeared and came back with a bottle of beautiful clear, pale green glass, handing it to her with a smile of triumph.

We filled the bottle with treasures from Dunstanborough, shells, stones, weeds, and of course some sharp, salt seawater, and the next time I visited my mother I gave it to her.

Many years afterwards she returned to live where her windows look out on the sea, and she can walk along her own beach. She's ninety-one now, but she still smiles each time I mention my friend's name. The pleasure of the gift remains.

Friendship is a part of my survival kit, packed along with faith and hope. Every so often I fall, and it is friendship that lifts me up. When I wander off the path it is friendship that seeks me, and guides me back. Friendship is that calm strong hand that takes hold and steadies you when you are frightened, weary or discouraged. It says "Hang on, you'll be alright, you can do it. I won't leave you."

Friends hear what you mean, even if it was not exactly what you said. Some friends I may meet only once, but in a moment's sharing we are no longer strangers. The gift has been given and received. Other friends are there through the years to double the joys, and be a bulwark against the pains and disappointments. Some loyalties may have been offered in an instant, a grace entirely unearned. Others I have labored for through difficulties, misunderstandings, little things shared, silly jokes and small achievements. These friendships are woven into the fabric

75

of my existence.

Friends show me the laughter and the beauty they have found in life because they want me to share it. They tell me of their victories, but they also allow me into their defeats and their sorrows, because they trust me to tread softly where there is pain. They permit me to give as well as to take.

Friends believe in my virtues, even when I do not believe in them myself, in fact particularly then. And I will strive with all my strength to live up to their trust. They are not blind to my faults, but continue to love me and touch the places that hurt with a gentle hand.

Love is a word too often misunderstood, and friendship is one not valued enough. Without friendship life would be too heavy a burden to bear, and if I could not be a friend, then it would be a gift I am not worthy to have, because I would not have begun to understand the world, or He who created it out of chaos, and gave it light and meaning.

Friendship is love; Love is friendship. It connects us to everything that matters. Without it we would be adrift.

As I work in a museum about war, I have had the privilege of learning about the unique nature of friendship which develops in time of conflict. Reading through the letters and diaries of servicemen, servicewomen, civilians and children, one sees that it is the enduring thread of friendship that keeps people going in the most difficult of circumstances.

Who can fail to be touched emotionally as the archive box is opened? We see the creases that reveal how often a precious letter from home was taken out from a battle dress pocket and read over and over again. The stilted hand writing on the page of a diary shows how the writer sat reflecting on the news of the death in action of a beloved friend, unable to put on paper the depth of feeling for someone who had shared a past but who will not be there to share in future dreams.

From these scraps of paper come the stories of how enduring friendships developed from a simple gesture: the cup of tea brought over to an exhausted soldier; the words of courage spoken as the shrapnel flew. Thrown together by chance, these people discovered a friendship that was to last through war and into peace.

Friendship in time of conflict is unique, and we should learn the value of it from the legacy of those who have experienced it.

I just finished reading the biography *John Adams* by David McCullough (New York Simon & Schuster, 2001) in which many friendships were depicted. But the one that reflects what I would like to consider as a true friendship was the one between John Adams and Dr. Benjamin Rush. Both were interested in the revolutionary politics going on at the time. It initially brought them together. Their friendship thrived despite geographic distance and very real differences in political views. They treated one another with respect. I think they trusted one another. I think they recognized and appreciated each other's uniqueness and counted this friendship as a treasure to be cultivated.

In the diet of life a friend should be both a staple and a dessert. Man is a social creature. Common things bring us together: geography, work, hobbies, disasters, marriages, politics, humor, etc. We develop friendships everywhere. Much of the superficial kind can be like indulging in a favorite dessert – enjoyable but not usually something we can count on for what we really need to sustain us. The real friendships—the staple of the diet—are the kind where concern for the other is the ruling force. They can count on us because we care about them.

Friendship is waking up in the morning and knowing you're not alone in the world.

Friendship is being able to turn up on your friend's doorstep at any time of night or day, for an unspecified period of time after a break-up of a relationship.

Friendship is someone picking you up at or taking you to the airport or bus or train station, at a time most inconvenient to them.

Friendship is not telling your friend "something they ought to know, or for their own good," when it could potentially hurt them.

Friendship is letting your friend be free without criticism or hindrance.

Friendship is going to stay with a friend in the midst of a crisis (yours) and then relaxing to the point of falling asleep when they're putting themselves out and driving around to show you the most stunning scenery, to help relax you, which it does beyond expectations. And they say nothing!

I think one of the greatest single acts of kindness and friendship shown to me was after my mother's very recent death, when one of my closest friends helped me sort and pack up my mother's flat, when I was completely alone and in the most vulnerable state I could be. There were all my mother's clothes and personal belongings, furniture, everything to be sorted and assigned their final destination. It took about ten hours, was the most heartrending and painful experience and my friend was practical and calm. I could not have done it without her.

Friendship is kindness, the smile on a person's face when they see you, and above all the knowledge that you can count on the friendship, which will be steadfast and true until the end of your lives.

NATIA MIKELADZE

SECOND YEAR ENGLISH STUDENT, TBILISI FOREIGN LANGUAGE INSTITUTE

Friendship means being friends. It is the feeling or relationship that exists between people. How good it is to live together in friendship; in a family, school or college, between neighbors and between countries. I can't imagine living without friends. I have many good friends. They are always ready to help me if I am in need and I always try to be there for them.

Friendship is very important throughout our life. There should be friendship between countries. Such a small country as Georgia needs supporters. We must be on friendly terms with other countries. Our government must try to have good relationships with other countries, especially with neighboring ones. There must be friendship between us and America, and between us and Russia. I think nowadays friendship is the most important thing. We don't only need it in a family or in the country, but all over the world, because it is of great importance and people need friendship everywhere.

81

The greatest good you can do for another is not just to share your riches, but to reveal to him his own.

My introduction to friendship bound by a common cause had its beginnings during Georgia's Civil War of 1991, shortly after the break-up of the Soviet Union. The necessity of having to stay indoors had begun to affect everyone. Safe places to visit were at a premium, so I readily agreed when I was invited to tour a nearby fire station.

What I saw there made me want to cry. Living quarters and kitchen areas were dismal. Antiquated fire trucks could easily be outrun by a person in good condition. Tires had no tread. Out-of-date, self-breathing oxygen tanks looked more like lethal weapons than life-saving instruments. Hoses, pumps, boots, and protective clothing appeared sadly inadequate.

Yet the poorly outfitted firefighters gathered around me responded to an average of sixty fires a day at serious risk to themselves. It was common knowledge that they refused to take sides in the present conflict and fought fires no matter where or how they started. Their dedication in the face of such odds was touching. Surely something could be done. As if from nowhere, I heard myself say in a perfectly calm voice, "One day I'll get you an American fire engine."

The words fell a long way into total silence. It was my heart which had spoken. My mouth had only framed the words, but they were too much for the interpreter who had accompanied me.

"How can you say that," he demanded. "Look at them. These people have been disappointed so often. Do you actually have a fire engine?"

"No."

"And if you had one, how would you get it here from halfway across the world?"

83

"Right now I have no idea, but it will all come together."

Shaking his head, the interpreter conveyed my message. He had a point. How could I have promised? All I knew about firefighters was that they were dedicated professionals willing to risk their lives for others when the need arose, and that the dogs in my neighborhood barked at the sound of their sirens.

The men were courteous in their response to my promise, yet a carefully monitored, unexpressed doubt showed in their eyes. And who could blame them? It was not every day a foreigner, and a woman at that, walked into the station and made a substantial, spur-of-the-moment commitment. Until recently Georgia had been a country with closed borders. The break-up of the Soviet Union was only a few weeks old. Soviet citizens as a whole had limited experience with visitors from capitalist countries, especially the United States. Those were barriers enough, even without considering the geographical and logistical obstacles which would need to be overcome for an American fire engine to reach their shores.

It was a lot to take on faith.

Reluctant to carry the burden of their disbelief, I searched for a way to convince them. I had already kicked two of the tires— as I had seen men at home do – but it told me absolutely nothing. Then I remembered that firefighters extended hoses by joining them with metal couplings. From there it was easy to recall that to prevent invasion, railroad tracks in the Soviet Union were built to a gauge different from those in the rest of Europe. Invasions and fire hoses had nothing in common, but it seemed reasonable that the diameter of a hose here might also be different from those at home. Would this present a problem? The men assured me they could adapt whatever they received.

With my question I must have passed some kind of test, because from that point on there was a subtle change in their interaction with me. The weight of distrust had been lightened.

After returning to Utah, I followed a well-established pattern of sharing some of my experiences with friends. Almost as an afterthought, I mentioned to one of them my promise of the fire engine. Her reply was equally casual. No question, no further comments. Like my other friends, she had long ago stopped being surprised by anything I did.

Responsibilities continued to take me in and out of Georgia. Occasional visits to the fire station always brought a friendly reception but never a question about the status of the truck. I would not have had an answer anyway. What I did have was an unshakable faith. Thinking about it logically rather than listening to my heart changed nothing. I was at peace with my commitment.

Two years after the initial conversation with my Utah friend, I was delighted when I learned that her daughter had become mayor of Salt Lake City. As I had not met Mayor Corradini, I was most surprised when a member of her staff telephoned to ask if I could use not only one, but two, twenty-year-old fire trucks. Government regulations required that both be taken out of service, he explained. I composed myself long enough to supply the information he needed to move the process along. Evening found me empty of tears but full of gratitude. Half of the promise had been realized.

The remaining challenge was to get the fire engines across the Atlantic, through the Black Sea, and overland to Tbilisi, the capital of Georgia. A humanitarian agency agreed to take on this task. Assistance came from other sources as well. Salt Lake City firemen entered wholeheartedly into the spirit of the project and used many of their free hours to wash, polish, and generously outfit the trucks.

Transporting the fire engines on two flatbed trailers to Texas was the easy part. The trucks left Utah without fanfare or media attention. The real odyssey began after they were secured on the open deck of a container vessel in the port of Houston. At one point during the voyage, the waves grew so high that the captain considered letting the engines go overboard. He did not, but they were encrusted with salt when the ship finely docked in the Black Sea harbor of Batumi. Any equipment not bolted down had long since disappeared.

Happy even with the stripped-down models, the firemen of Tbilisi proudly drove them into the city with lights flashing and sirens blaring. It was indeed a cause for celebration. To honor the givers, the Salt Lake City logo was left on the doors.

The men soon familiarized themselves with every detail of the trucks. Their expertise proved particularly useful when an assassination attempt destroyed President Edward Shevardnadze's seven car motorcade. The Salt Lake City fire engines were the first on the scene.

Given the prominence of the Georgian President, the event was televised worldwide. No one was more surprised than the crew of a Salt Lake City television station. Viewing the video feed for the evening news, they saw the injured president standing in front of a Salt Lake City fire engine. One can imagine the questions voiced at that moment. If the president was in Utah, how could they not have known? If he was in his own country, how could a Salt Lake City fire truck be in the former Soviet Union? While the crew was still trying to make sense of it, a second Salt Lake City fire engine drove into view.

The Georgian embassy in Washington, D.C., soon shed light on the matter and the quiet good deed of the Salt Lake City Mayor was broadcast on worldwide television.

Since that time the bonds of friendship have been strengthened as firemen from Utah have visited, worked with, taught and learned from their Georgian counterparts. With newborn faith in themselves and their abilities, Georgia's firemen have opened a clinic to take care of the medical needs of their own families and those of walk-ins.

One rented-out section of the fire-services building now contains a popular restaurant operated by a former colleague; this one a refugee from an earlier conflict. Another part houses a copy center, also for public use. Initiative and determination are changing conditions for the better.

Mother Teresa believed that "we can

do no great things, only small things with great love." Many selfless individuals eased the burden of valiant firefighters in a little-known corner of the globe. At every step, good hearted people smoothed the way and contributed means and ideas to help achieve the goal. And as is customary among friends, assistance was given without expecting recognition or reward.

The loss of the fire truck's tools was regrettable, but it could have been worse. I was surprised to learn that one thousand containers fall overboard every year from ships on the high seas. Perhaps it was better to have any subsequent vehicles transported by plane. With luck I would obtain more fire engines, but where to get a plane big enough to carry such a load.

The answer came from a friend in Washington. "What you need is a C-5A Galaxy! It's one of the world's largest aircraft, big enough to hold one hundred Volkswagen Beetles. Transporting some trucks will not be a problem," he informed me. "Your project may well qualify for the Denton Program, put in the papers and see what happens."

We met the criteria of the Denton humanitarian assistance program, which permits the Air Force to transport without charge and when space is available, supplies donated by non-governmental sources. And yes, we would get a C-5A. A number of them were located at Kelly Air Force Base, Texas. If I could find a crew willing to go on this mission we would be on our way.

Members of the 433rd Airlift wing answered the request and were generous enough to give of their time and talent. They would pick up and then deliver what friends and I had gathered.

At times coordinating everything felt like threading a needle. Especially after a U.S. Government official decided that we could not use the Georgian airstrip because no C5-Galaxy had ever landed there. International specifications showed that it was safe enough, but his way of thinking remained firm.

With refueling stops in Maryland and at bases in both Spain and Turkey, our final destination would be Yerevan, Armenia, all told a journey of approximately sixty-one hours. The official's verdict also meant that I would have to ask Georgian firemen to drive to Yerevan, load the contents onto trucks, and then return to Tbilisi across some rough, mountainous terrain. Over the years, these Georgians and I had established a relationship of trust. They would evenhandedly distribute the humanitarian aid to their fellow citizens.

Though we had never discussed the subject I knew that initially the firefighters would have preferred to have a man come to their rescue. I felt it and decided to ignore it, hoping things would change and they had. They now took fierce pride in our ability to work together.

The day of the U.S. team's scheduled departure was February 27th. Weather conditions at Kelly, Texas were not good; high winds at Hill Air Force Base in Ogden, Utah created problems serious enough for the freeway to be closed. All planes were grounded. But by now ten Georgian trucks had left for Yerevan. With snow on the passes it would take them two days to get there and I had no way to call them back.

My feelings must have been evident to a battle-toughened sergeant.

"Everything will be all right, honey," he

said. "We're going to do this. Don't lose sleep over it. Sometimes you have to spit at the devil's feet and let him know your intentions!"

There was no time to lose sleep anyway and my intentions were to get the cargo safely delivered, but the enormity of the project weighed heavily on me. I had an emotional connection to Georgia; members of the crew would leave their families and fly half-way across the world on a voluntary basis.

A Utah television unit planned to document the journey. Also present on the trip were two Salt Lake City firemen, making it a total of twenty-two people.

In the end it worked out just as the sergeant had predicted. The weather improved and we were cleared to go.

It was a thrill to watch the loading of fire trucks, ambulances and other humanitarian aid into the belly of the huge aircraft. And then we took off, comfortably seated inside a plane almost as long as a football field and as high as a six-story building.

I could not believe its size. Someone had conceived it, built it, and now it was being used to bring help to people in another country; humanity at its best.

Throughout the planning stage I had told the Texas crew about Georgian hospitality and how guests and friends are welcomed there. We had looked forward to this experience; instead, we ate by the side of the runway while the cargo was being off-loaded. With only three hours before the plane needed to start the return trip, this was the best we could do. But my Georgian friends had come prepared. They were determined to share a meal with the American team and if that meant grilling

Shish Kebab right there on the premises so be it.

It was a unique beginning of a friendship. We would meet again, though for now we had responsibilities in different areas.

We were almost back in Georgia when the brakes on one of our trucks overheated. The driver wisely pulled off the road, but could not save the vehicle from tipping over on the steep S-curve. Some of its cargo of beans, dried milk etc., spilled down the hillside only yards away, but since everything was fairly well packaged, the loss was minimal. And more importantly, no one was hurt. Someone in a passing car promised to alert authorities to our problem.

The first crane to arrive was not big enough to raise the truck, even after it had been totally unloaded, which meant that we had time for another picnic. A number of drivers stopped to ask what was going on, especially after they saw the truck lying on its side and the television crew at work. Not wanting to admit that one of their own had run into trouble on a hill in Armenia, my Georgian friends calmly explained that "an American company was filming an important documentary." After a while it became difficult for me to keep a straight face.

The rest of the trip passed without incident. We rolled into Tbilisi seven hours late, grateful for a good ending.

I had promised the San Antonio flight crew the kind of feast for which the Georgians are deservedly famous and they would get it; only it would now to be at a different time. All I had to do was gather more items.

Plans were well on the way once someone back east decided it made sense to have the Tbilisi runway surveyed so a large plane could land there should the need arise in the future.

The kindness of people has ever been a humbling experience for me. Six months later I had enough vehicles and food items to fill another C-5A. To my delight, most of the original Texas group signed on again. And this time they would fly into Tbilisi. A large Georgian contingent met the plane when it arrived. Givers and receivers alike looked forward to getting better acquainted. We were waving to each other before the aircraft had even stopped.

When the pilot raised the American flag in the open cargo hold there was not a dry eye among us. At a banquet later that day, we celebrated friendship and a job well done. And for a change, my countrymen left laden with presents, sufficient to have another celebration when they reached home.

Given the world situation, I knew it would be impossible to send more trucks to Georgia, by plane anyway, yet the need for these emergency vehicles remained.

While on a business trip to Germany, I asked a staff member of the Düsseldorf Mayor's office what they did with their old fire engines, and if it was at all possible to obtain one truck when it was replaced with a new vehicle.

I had asked for one; within a matter of weeks I had Mayor Erwin's promise of seven fire engines and two ambulances. Such generosity was overwhelming, to say the least, but I believed the offer would become a reality and made the necessary arrangements.

Some months later, ten Georgian firefighters and I met in Düsseldorf, were made welcome by members of the fire department, generously outfitted with tools, uniforms and provisions for the trip, had the gas tanks filled to the top, and then we were on our own. From my place in the last vehicle the convoy was an impressive sight.

We reached the outskirts of Nürnberg in the evening of the first day. I had forgotten that a German law prohibits trucks over a certain size and weight from using the Autobahn on Sundays. This rule leaves the freeway clear for passenger cars. For us it meant a day's enforced rest at an Aral Gas Station. The only escape from the bitter cold was a coffee shop. The employees were helpful and friendly; even more so when they learned about our mission. They treated us to dessert and allowed us to stay indoors, rather than have us wait long hours in the chilly vehicles.

We were able to leave at ten p.m., and headed south through snowstorms and rain squalls like a determined caterpillar.

To stay awake my fireman had the radio blaring at its accustomed level, but this time the volume was turned up at my request. Through the static and crackling of a poor reception, came a by now familiar voice.

"We would like to dedicate this song to the members of the firefighter convoy driving toward Venice. This is from your friends at the Aral Station."

The song was "Goodbye San Francisco," but it was exactly right for us. We knew what it meant: Friendship—Bread for the Journey.

DSP

At the age of forty-seven I packed seven suitcases, took my six-year-old son and my crazy dog and jumped on a plane to start a new life in the United States. All of my family and friends were in Germany. I had no idea what I could expect or what would happen.

Soon I became a member of the Newcomer's Club and met some very nice people. We play golf, go skiing, play bridge or just visit. Some of them have become really good friends. What happened with my friends in Germany? Long distance phone calls, a few letters and some visits. Friendship can exist over a long distance, but I found out very soon who my real friends were.

People are different in different countries.

In Germany you sometimes stay up the whole night long and discuss politics. I've not had any discussions like that here. We talk more about family and barbecue and have lots of fun. Friends are easy-going here. In Germany it takes a while to warm up. What do I like better? There is no better. Friends are friends. I think fifteen years ago my best friend was my dog. He was always with me. But then of course this was a totally different kind of friendship.

Would I like to go back? I don't think so. I miss my family, but I started a new life with new friends and I stay in touch with my old friends. Having friends all over the world is very important for me and keeps me going.

*F*riendship adds quality and depth to one's life.

JONATHAN HULME, PHYSICIAN
M.A., B.M., B.CH. (OXON)

he patient I had been called to see was a well-educated, attractive young African woman. Her mother was a minister in President Mugabe's government, and her late father was one of the liberation heroes of the Third World. I was an ex-Rhodesian army doctor, and more interested in guns, gunshot wounds and broken bones than in eating disorders in over privileged young females. But Zine was quite a character. She was intelligent, manipulative and pressuring in the nicest possible way, with plenty of charm and charisma.

That was when she was in form, but when she was depressed, she was a pathetic piece of humanity. She talked, I listened, and we overcame the gaps of age, race, politics and culture and got on famously. Information that she had withheld from other doctors who were much more qualified than I, she divulged.

I considered myself privileged, but I was not experienced at handling manic-depressive, anorexic-bulimic Zulu princesses! I knew what the medical treatment should be—that was the easy part—but I also had my ideas as to what space Zine needed to re-orientate her life, and that brought me into conflict with her mother! She would not allow Zine to leave Zimbabwe and insisted she remain under her protection as a dutiful cripple.

I did not see Zine's future like that. I had faith that with the right treatment she could and would become a whole human being. Her mother and I argued, but neither of us would budge! She had political clout and I did not! I received death threats, was banned by the Ministry of Health from even seeing the patient, and also reported to Mugabe himself. However, with the help of a colleague, and my usual unflappable sense of humor, we managed to thwart the system and get Zine to London where, mercifully, she got the appropriate treatment.

The transformation was miraculous. What pleased me more than anything was to see the hatred that a daughter had for her mother turned into love. Through Zine I had seen into the deepest recesses of someone else's soul and seen their fragile and desperate attempts to hold everything together. And I had learned much about myself in the process. I gained respect, self-respect and courage, and I had truly earned a friend. It was a right of passage. For what I had done for Zine I did not want thanks, or even acknowledgment. We had joined in a liberation struggle, and we were winners.

Through the years we could phone each other or e-mail, and pick up the conversation where we had left off, and catch up on each other's news. There was an ease in our relationship. What the future would hold for Zine, I did not know, but I did not believe she would ever have to go through those traumas again. The man she was due to marry died, leaving her to bring up a daughter by herself.

Straightforward disasters like that she coped with very well. But family pressures began to mount, and fifteen years after I had met her, she finally succeeded in killing herself. I was immensely sad. I felt that if I had stayed in Zimbabwe, this would not have happened, but my family and I had left, to escape the political and financial disasters of Mugabe. Much as I believe in the freedom of people to choose their lives, I wish I could have been there for my friend. I had sweated blood to keep her alive before but that was not the issue. She deserved better. For what

I gave her and what I received, I am grateful and enriched. I have lost a special friend, but Zine's mother has lost a daughter, and Zine's daughter has lost a mother.

Losing people this way is not exactly careless, but knowing how to care more is not easy. It requires an honesty, sensitivity and encouragement; sometimes a humility and sometimes an arrogance. How wise was I to take all those risks for a friend? I think it is the only wisdom worth having and the only risks worth taking.

Tucked away in a sheltered cove on Oregon's rugged coast, there is a small community. Those looking for a resort town will be sadly disappointed, for there are no stores, no hotels, or special services. But for those loving the sea and a piece of solitude it is an ideal place.

A little more than a hundred yards from the sea stands a small house. Unpretentious on the outside, and comfortably furnished, it has been home away from home for many years. Pages of life as well as novels have been written here, for this is a house where friendship dwells; a place where memories and anticipation hold hands and feel equally at home.

Its windows look out over the vast Pacific, offering limitless views of sea and sky. Within its walls, one feels safe and secure, no matter how wild the wind or fierce the storms. Friendship is not unlike that house on the coast. Unpretentious and accommodating, true friendship is a haven, a safe place where there's always room for encouragement and time to listen. Laughter with a friend is much like a fresh sea breeze, it clears the mind. The furnishings of friendship never cater to fashion, yet they are always in style. Like that limitless view of the Pacific, friendship's windows see clearly, allowing for faults and failings as well as strength. Yet somehow, they only mirror back a vision of our best selves.

Friendship is kind. Like a favorite chair, friendship offers comfort for the aches of life and quietly acknowledges the pain. Occasionally, misunderstanding may enter uninvited, but it never stays long. Sharing and caring however are always welcome.

99

I first met Barbara when we were in the Liederkranz Foundation Vocal Competition award together in New York. Barbara was singing 'Butterfly' and I 'La Traviata'. Barbara showed me her footwear as Cio Cio San and we both laughed as she wore a size nine shoe and did a keen imitation of 'Thumper' in Mr. Walt Disney's 'Bambi'. Our next encounter was when I asked her to substitute for me at an Opera Club called Bianchi and Margherita in Greenwich Village.

From that day forward we became close friends. We found we could share anything with each other, good or bad, funny or awful, even if it was three o'clock in the morning.

The years passed and we saw many happy times and some painful ones together. Her boyfriend Ed, a most wonderful and kind man, died. My beloved daughter Maria passed away at the age of twenty-five years, from a long illness.

Through those dark days my friend was always there for me and I hope I was there for her. I now live in England and quite often am traveling with the opera group I direct. A dear member of my family is old and suffering from dementia, and it is Barbara I rely on to be there when I cannot, and to think of and do everything for him that I would. When I go to New York the years roll back and we are twenty-four years old again.

Friendship is an anchor which has helped stabilize my life. Friends are valuable to me. One of my favorite ways to spend an evening is to invite six diverse, but compatible, friends to my home for dinner and a lively visit. Cultivating a variety of friends, including those in my immediate and extended family, has provided me a foundation of security. I love the simulation of developing friendships with many types of people, and I value what they teach me.

Friends multiply my store of knowledge in the most pleasant ways. I can hardly wait to see an attorney friend when I have read about a legal issue and have questions. I solved many of the world's problems with a dear friend when we walked together in the mornings. My son, a biochemist, sent me a book titled DNA for Beginners so we could converse intelligently about his work. Three of my friends who are outstanding students of the scriptures open up my mind and pour in their understanding.

There is so much I want to learn, and with friends I am free to ask questions and to be nurtured in an encouraging way. I can provide the setting for this in my home or in the park or in a car on the way to a symphony performance. It doesn't take an expensive menu or a lavish centerpiece. I have had some wonderful conversations over curdly soup and rolls that have burned on the outside and are doughy in the middle. I've had a fascinating discussion about a trip to the bird refuge with my grandson over

101

a peanut butter and jelly sandwich. I could not live in isolation. I respond to family and friends. They encourage me, they buoy me up, they make me feel worthwhile. Friends are gifts from the Lord.

I have a bookmark which reads "Good friends and good books. Things we want to hang onto forever." Friends make life important, and need to be kept close.

The Lifeboat Service is the most exclusive club in Britain. When you go round the coast and call in at other stations, you meet friends, some that you have met before, and some not. These are people you work closely with and can rely on without any doubt, people who back you up. We are all in the service to help others.

103

It was through friendship that I joined the Invergordon lifeboat crew in 1983, being invited out by the coxswain of the boat.

After a short time I became the full-time mechanic, joining the rest of the crew who are all volunteers. Some of us have been together on station for many years, new blood joining as others retire. We have bonded as a firm team, we train together to do our job of saving life at sea, we trust and help each other, out of work-time, at work, and even socialize together. If this can be done within the lifeboat crew over my twenty year experience, that's a pretty good friendship.

Friendship is a vital part of being on the lifeboat crew. You must have complete trust and faith in the crew when on a 'shout'. Situations can vary and can often be dangerous and upsetting. You have to know that whatever the situation or outcome you will have unfaltering support from your friends.

After a long hard search in difficult conditions, going back to the crew room and having a wee dram and a chat, or even sitting in silence, is the best therapy there is. It is almost like having one big family.

105

Friendship is about knowing someone will be there to help you pull on the rope that is too strong for you. It is about being empowered to feel comfortable with yourself, your strengths and weaknesses. It is about learning new skills and getting unconditional tuition and support when you fail.

It is about teaching and imparting knowledge to those who want to learn to help others, showing that they care what you try to teach them.

It is listening and laughing, sharing experiences and smiling. It is about crying and helping others to express emotions without fear of ridicule.

It is about bonding and caring in a quiet, understated way. It is the hand that gives you a drink and mops up your vomit when you are too ill to move.

It is about feeling part of the team, of being scared but trusting each other to pull through.

It is about going into a room where everyone knows your name. Mostly it is about wanting to be on a 'shout' because they are your friends and you cannot let them down.

During the Civil War my great-uncle's son, George, was drafted into the Confederate army during the war between the states. The son took off, rather than join the army. He was terrified. My great-uncle found him, talked to him, and saw that his son just did not have the heart for the war.

My great-uncle, George Lansdale, Sr., to keep the boy from going to prison, rode into the Confederate lines, and took George, Jr.'s place without any great hullabaloo. Since they were both George Lansdale, and George Lansdale had been drafted, no one ever knew there had been a swap. My great-uncle, at that time, was over fifty years old. He served throughout the war, and in the end, returned to Texas only to be killed a few years later during a misunderstanding over the sale of a horse.

A sad end to a noble gentleman, who loved his son, and sacrificed years of his life to keep his son from having to serve, and possibly be slain in combat. For my taste, that's the kind of love, the kind of friendship you can't beat.

$\mathcal{D}$eep friendships take time or a crisis to develop, but even a casual friendship can add color and warmth to an ordinary day. When driving along the road in Idaho with Clyde, my six-foot-four, two-hundred-eighty pound co-driver, we passed an older sedan on the shoulder of the freeway. I noticed some fluid had been dripping on the pavement just behind the car. I mentioned it to my partner and we began to slow down, wondering if the people needed our help. Before we had decided, the car pulled onto the interstate, accelerated, and passed us, smoking like a coal burning railroad engine. The car then pulled to the side of the road, and an elderly lady jumped out and flagged us down.

The driver of the car was also somewhere in her late sixties. We learned that they were both widows, and on their way to one of their favorite fishing holes when the transmission began to act up. The driver of the car was quiet and reserved. The passenger was outgoing and enthusiastic. The women probably complemented each other very well. We checked under their car and transmission fluid was leaking onto the exhaust pipe and catalytic converter, hence all the smoke.

We told them about the next town, where there might be a mechanic or at least a tow truck. They asked if we would follow them there in case they had trouble on the way and we agreed. When their car would not start, we suggested they come with us in the truck. The driver insisted on staying with her vehicle, her friend readily agreed to ride with us.

On the way the woman said her son, who always worried about her independence, would not believe she had driven in a huge truck with strangers. We arrived in the town, spoke with the owner of the truck-stop and introduced the lady to him. We had a throw away camera and took a few pictures of her in the truck and promised to send them to her once they were developed. My co-driver and I laughed together about this outgoing woman, and how great that she was doing all the things she wanted to do. Fishing, traveling, etc.—it was a good attitude to have. We also decided to get some additional pictures to send to her so she could have some fun with her son. We found the biggest, ugliest, and hairiest truck driver we could find and took a few photos of him.

When we got back to the Frito-Lay plant a week or so later, we found she had written a thank you note to our boss. The experience had been a pleasant, friendly encounter appreciated by all.

JEFFREY MEER
EXECUTIVE DIRECTOR, UNITED NATIONS ASSOCIATION FOR U.N. H. C. R.

once had a friend who found me when I was lost and brought me home.

I once had a friend, who, without even asking, brought me hot chicken soup when I was ill and all alone.

I once had a friend who unhesitatingly volunteered to write a letter of recommendation for me for a job even though he didn't agree with the organization's viewpoint.

I once had a friend who took time off from his job in Maryland to bring my family home from the airport in Virginia after a long international trip.

I once had a friend who drove more than fifty miles at night to pick me up when my car broke down on the New York State Thruway.

For all of these friends, and for the many others who have helped, guided, provided and otherwise supported me through the years, I am and will always be deeply grateful. A world without friendship would be a cold, lonely and desolate place.

The Friend

Let me be the hearth
Where you sit to work your clay.
I'll not say
"Shape it like this or like that,"
I promise.

Let me watch
As you in absolute agency
Mold your mortal dream.

Only sit close
And let me give a little light,
A little warmth.
Yes, warmth especially.

Cold clay yields to no form.
Let me be your hearth.
Sit close.
Be warm.

111

I remember her name—Blanche. I vaguely remember her physique. She was large and seemed to be dragged down by layers of droopy skin. Something else about her seemed strange to me, the preschooler. Blanche had only one breast. I didn't, of course, know that then. I only knew that her clothes looked funny—pouched out on one side and flat on the other.

Her hair was short and grayish black, but I don't remember her face. She's faceless to me, just as she apparently was to other people years and years ago. Other people, except my mother. Mother brought Blanche home one day—Blanche and her five children. Where they came from, I never knew. Maybe I never asked. Maybe I was too young to care.

The occurrence was not, after all, unusual. Blanche was merely one (or should I say one through six?) of the seemingly countless numbers of downtrodden and distraught who shared our small house. Either they found us or mother found them. She'd help them through their immediate crisis and then they'd be gone, sometimes nearly as quickly as they came, and other times not nearly soon enough.

Blanche, who had breast cancer and no family or friends in the area, wasn't with us long. I don't know what became of her and her children, but I do know that Mom wouldn't have turned them out without a plan. I wish that I could remember Blanche's face. The fact that I can't is a little frightening to me and symbolic of the way we treat scores of unfortunate people today. Our response to them, if we respond at all, is often to write out a check to an equally nondescript organization. Our duty is done; our consciences are clear. Better yet our involvement, physically and emotionally, is nil.

In mom's day, there were few agencies and charities to take care of the indigent, the sick, the lonely. As the old saying goes, "Charity begins at home." It did, and only now do I realize what a singular person and friend my mother was and how better the world would be if more of us were able to recognize not problems but faces.

The man did not look Italian nor did he look European. At first I thought the rose vendor was just another illegal immigrant trying to scrounge a living. "A rose?" he asked. Had I been a little less thoughtless I would have immediately realized that he did not speak Italian. I would later find out that he did not speak English either. Trying to help him, I bought three roses for some ladies who were sitting at my table. I also asked where he was from, which he understood, answering he was from Pakistan. "So what is your name?"

"My name is Azhaar." He did not know how to ask me so he just pointed his finger at me. I told him that my name is Seba. "Seba!" He smiled and added, "Amico!" which means friend in Italian. It still is one of the only Italian words Azhaar knows, but it is a very good word. When I paid him he gave me four roses. "There's a mistake", I said, handing him back the fourth unpaid for flower. "I only paid for three..." He shook his head and did not take the flower. "Seba..., Amico!"

I happened to bump into him late one evening in one of the local bars. This guy must have been in his late twenties and had the smile of a seven-year-old child who had just been touched by a loving mother. And to think that each night he would catch a train from a bigger city and make a one and a half hour trip just to sell a bunch of flowers to people who often mock and insult him; a stranger in a world of strangers. Then, each morning he would catch a train back to the city he'd come from, after spending some hours sleeping on an uncomfortable chair in the railway station waiting room. And now here I was, a "friend" among a throng of strangers.

One night he saw me carrying my guitar and asked me in very awkward Italian whether I was going to give a concert and what sort of music I was into. I tried my best to tell him and was it ever hard. But he understood and managed to tell me he'd provide me with some music from Pakistan. I thought that was very kind of him. When I met him again in the main square the next night he almost ran toward me, excited as he was to give to me what he had promised to give me: two original tapes of the best-known Pakistani singer, Nusrat Fateh Ali Khan. This man, who did not have a fixed income and led a difficult life, was giving me something precious, something he might have been working hard to buy. I was very impressed, I was certainly moved. So I thought I'd do something for him. But what? From time to time I'd invite him over to my table and offer him a drink, obviously nonalcoholic. I also tried to make him feel comfortable at my table and so did my friends. And he would always give me roses for free. He would not accept money in return because he would say, "Seba…, Amico!" So I felt I needed to do something more to counterbalance his astounding generosity.

A friend of mine owns a bookshop and I asked him if he had an Italian-Urdu grammar book. Azhaar needed to speak our language if he really wanted to live in our country and obtain regular documents and a residence permit. He had told me that he was the last of ten children, that his mother had died and his father was an old man in Punjab, a region that borders India. I also learned that he had left his wife and two-year-old daughter in Pakistan and that he had been wandering in Europe and the Middle East in search of an occupation and of a job. He was willing to bring his family here too.

I ordered what I thought was a grammar book, only to find out that it was a huge collection of cards bearing an image and the Italian, English and Urdu word for it. More of a child's game than a real useful tool, but better than nothing! When I gave it to him at our usual haunt, he was thrilled, ecstatic I'd say. He would not stop smiling, thanking me and showing everybody in the bar those silly cards, proudly pointing at me and telling them the same old magical words: Seba…, Amico!"

Azhaar is a man, a good man. We've known each other for just a few months now and I don't know whether this is enough to call him a true friend. But he never seemed to have the same reserve. His friendship is unconditional. I was his "Amico" from the very first, just because I treated him like a man, considering him the human being he is.

I do not know whether I'll be able to help him find a job, although I'm trying, but I know I've learned something precious from him.

Friendship has meant many things over the years to me. From the very intense childhood friendships we feel will last forever until our lives diverge and they're gone, the memory lingers for a lifetime, to another kind of friendship I developed with my colleagues of the Clearance Diving Branch of the Royal Navy. This is where experience taught me that lives can depend on the trust built up between friends, who would certainly die for each other, and on rare occasions did.

We trained together in some of the hardest training regimes of any of the world's Armed Forces; courses where only three out of fourteen that started finished. On another more advanced course, forty-two started and only three of us finished after six months. This is where I developed unique friendships that defy description. We would, without thought, go to the aid of a friend, no matter what the circumstances or danger involved. In some way we developed a sixth sense as this story illustrates.

While working in 330 feet of water in the English Channel to recover a crashed SeaKing helicopter, my co-diver and friend George Gill and I left the diving bell to secure a lifting wire around the rotor head of the helicopter. The part was lying on its side one hundred feet away from the diving bell, which meant we were outside the arc of the bell lights. This operation was extremely dangerous.

To attach the lifting cable, we positioned ourselves on either side of the rotor head. While passing the cable between us around the rotor head, the groundswell moved the helicopter and pinned us both to the seabed by our shoulders. In that moment we did not realize we were both trapped, yet we both

117

thought, as later discussion revealed, that the swell that moved the airframe would probably do so again and allow us to free ourselves.

For five minutes, which seemed like an eternity, unable to help or speak to each other, we shared the silent conviction that we would survive. I knew that my friend was exactly in the same situation, feeling the same as I did, trapped the way I was. He would be thinking of me just as I was thinking of him.

Back in 1972 there was no voice communication with each other or the surface, so it was our friendship and trust that saved our lives, helping us to remain calm and in control, with enough confidence not to panic.

The incident was unknown to the crew of the mother vessel above us, who by this time were concerned that we had not returned, and feared for our lives as our air supply was almost exhausted. As we had hoped, the ground swell came again, lifted the air frame and allowed us to escape.

The experience created a bond that has never been forgotten. Life is about friendship, the very reason for our lives is to teach us how to befriend our fellow man.

believe I've enjoyed friendship a lot in my life, and for that I count myself blessed. There is nothing more enjoyable than sharing time with a friend, and isn't that what life is all about, finding joy? And if not finding it, then surely giving joy to a friend.

Of all those I have experienced so far, the purest friendship I have witnessed took place at the Hospital Burn Unit.

Of the many hundreds of severe burns that I have worked with, the case of one young man stands out above the rest. He was burned over 95 percent of his body, after falling into a 'hot pot' at Yellowstone National Park. Two of his friends were burned more severely than he, one surviving and one passing away. The friendship I witnessed brings tears to my eyes even now. The incredible outpouring of love and support from people all over the country was truly amazing. He had dozens of friends writing in a book, wishing him well and leaving touching thoughts for their injured friend. His mother, who was ever by his side, would read their words to him during therapy on days when we stretched his scarred skin, in hopes of returning function and independence to his life. For many weeks, it was unclear whether he would live or not, but as time passed it became obvious that his will to live, and give back, would win.

119

What he gave was hope. Lying in bed, with cultured (scientifically grown) skin covering about 20 percent of his body, he smiled. He talked about the future and how he would be a better person for having undergone this trial in his life. He strengthened all of us. It was a joy to work with him. As terrible as his injury was, and as hard as it was to watch him and his friend go through the pain and suffering a major burn can give, he gave me joy. I felt good going home at night. It felt good to share his story. Even though I cannot claim to be his friend, I felt a touch of the friendship he gave to all, and that will suffice. I'll never forget my time with him and his mother.

I will never forget the strength he showed, and the hope he has given my life. The challenges we endure are unique to each of us, but will surely grant us some opportunity to surprise the world when we smile despite our suffering. If we are strong enough, perhaps we can touch the life of one person, and show them that life is what we make of it. It can be done. I've seen it. I only hope for the strength to share the joy that pure friendship has shown to me.

The willingness to overlook issues of less importance and concentrate on the essential is the hallmark of a wise person. George Eliot said that "the responsibility of tolerance lies with those who have the wider vision."

One of my friends has made this attribute her own. Throughout nearly two decades of friendship, I have observed her as consistently accepting of all people, embracing them with her words and her presence. An incident which took place some time ago is evidence of her ability to draw from the wisdom of both head and heart.

I was involved in a time-consuming, complex project. Although there had been occasional difficulties, my co-workers and I had dealt with them and moved on—or so I thought until it became clear that certain decisions and even my integrity were being questioned.

At first furious and then hurt, I felt betrayed. My father had given me his name in good condition, and I was not about to let it be damaged.

Though I cared passionately for the goals of the project, at that moment abandoning the effort looked extremely enticing. But before taking this drastic step, I wanted to talk with my friend. I looked to her for advice, judgment, and approval. As always, she listened without interrupting and then offered incisive council.

"What is gained by giving up," she asked. "Think of the consequences. You can resolve this. I don't doubt it for a minute. The question is whether you want to."

She was right. I did not want to resolve the problem, nor did I want to hear that I should. Blinded by hurt, I could not find tolerance in my vocabulary. Nevertheless, faced with her calm expectation that those around her do the best they are capable of, I headed her advice, and immediately felt better for having done so.

The whole experience reinforced what I already knew. My friend, the much-loved matriarch of an extensive family, is fluent in the enlightened language of wisdom. In her it is an everyday quality.

I affectionately call her the Swan. Demands on her are considerable, yet she glides from one requirement to another with elegance and poise. More than once I have asked her how she meets the challenge of her diverse roles. The answer is always the same: she evaluates the situation, decides on a goal, and works toward it, letting it drift through the nets of her understanding things of little worth and holding fast those that enrich and make a difference.

I am grateful to have friends who comfortably rely on the wisdom of both head and heart. So much can be gained and so much lost without it. It is no wonder Solomon asked for this rare gift.

DSP

Being an Indian-American, I have heard countless anecdotes about India from all members of my family. My father once told me this true story about my grandfather, or as I call him, Tatagaru, and his best friend growing up. My Tatagaru has lived in India since he was born and has experienced much in his life that most of us could not imagine. His family taught him to be a devout Hindu and follow tradition, yet there was a time when he broke this barrier just because of a significant friendship he felt was more important.

An integral and often inhibiting piece of India in history has always been the caste system. Stemming from India's dominant religion of Hinduism, this rigid social structure has been a part of society for centuries. From the Brahmins at the top of the hierarchy descending to the harijans at the bottom, the caste system dictates class divisions, most often bringing prejudice along with it. Specifically, the traditionally low harijans, or as they are more popularly known, the "Untouchables," have always suffered from discrimination, mostly from the upper classes. They are often forced to do menial labor tasks that rarely allow them to be treated with respect, just because of the social status. Although this has improved somewhat in modern times, when my grandfather was young, the caste system was very much an important part of life.

Years ago, my Tatagaru's best friend was a harijan. Tatagaru, however, is a Brahmin. As they were young, these class distinctions bothered them little, and they spent most of their adolescence growing up together. After graduating from school, my grandfather took his father's job as owner of the family farm. His best friend, on the other hand, being

123

a harijan, was not hired anywhere else. He had no choice but to follow his own father and become a laborer. As life would have it, he started working for his best friend, my Tatagaru, on his farm.

Years passed and times changed, and my grandfather and his friend both married and gained families. Even though they worked in such close proximity, the two never spent time together. Tatagaru's family would not allow his friend to even enter the house, and looked down on him plainly because of his caste. His friend was never permitted to speak to my grandfather because he was his employee and an "Untouchable." If Tatagaru ever walked in front of him, his friend had to take off his shoes and could not look directly at his face. These class divisions tore them further and further apart, yet they never forgot each other.

Now my grandfather's friend had a son. As tradition has shown, the boy would have to follow his father into the fields. When my grandfather found this out, however, he refused. This boy reminded him of the past when he and his friend were young and sincere, innocent and oblivious to the realities of life. Tatagaru went to his friend and told him that he would take in his son and educate him himself. He said that the boy was like his own son, and he did not want history to repeat itself and deny his son all he was capable of. My grandfather boldly defied tradition and took in his best friend's son, a harijan, because he wanted to give him a chance to succeed in a society that would not allow him to.

Today this boy is a renowned professor at a prestigious engineering college in India.

During his frequent visits to Tatagaru,

my grandfather treats him like his own son. He is extremely proud of how far he has come in life. If the boy is ever mentioned in conversation, my grandfather is the first to boast about his accomplishments. My Tatagaru never got another chance to spend time with his best friend, which he deeply regrets. Yet he feels that by watching over his son, he is making up their lost time together.

People who work on ocean tugs are sometimes at sea for five or six months at a time. The ability to get along in close quarters is a must. Compatibility is cast in stone, from the captain down. The sixteen or seventeen people on board know within twenty-four hours what a person's beliefs are, and what their hygienic status is.

Things can happen in a hurry. Crises develop. It's a life or death dependency.

One time I was with a crew who took three towboats, the kind you see on the Mississippi, from the United States to the Mekong Delta, and taught some Vietnamese boatmen how to operate them. It was a challenge as we did not speak their language, nor did they speak ours, but somehow we managed. During some of those extraordinary experiences I made friends I have never lost.

126

I remember when I was young, about twelve years old. I used to hang out at this place called the Hobo Jungle. It was a wooded area on the outskirts of my neighborhood.

We kids were told not to go down there, but I didn't get along with my dad and brothers, so I would hang out there to see what the hobos were doing.

I finally got enough courage to talk to one of them and he invited me into his camp. He was easygoing and shared what he had with me and we just sat around and talked. Then I told him I had to go, but if he wanted I would come back the next day. He said yes. On my way home, all I could think about was going again the next day and when I did, I waited for everyone to be out of the house, so I could sneak some potatoes and canned goods to take to the hobo's camp.

When I got close I hollered, "Hello in the camp, I'm a friend," and one of the hobos invited me in. He asked, "Hey, young fellow, whatcha got?" I said, "I have some potatoes and canned goods for us to eat."

With a cautious smile on his face he asked, "Where did you get them?"

I said, "From my mom," and he said, "You didn't steal them from your house, did you?"

I lied and said, "No, my mom gave it to me," and he said, "Your Ma's okay with you hanging out down here?"

Again I lied and said, "Yeah, my dad's okay with it too." So he had me run and get some water from the river so we could cook the food.

After doing this for a while I started to get to know him more and we became friends, to where I didn't have to say, "Hello in the camp," anymore, I could just come in.

127

I also got to know more hobos. There were lots of them 'cause the rail-yards were next to the river and the Hobo Jungle.

I was known as the "young fellow" in the Hobo Jungle and I had lots of friends there. My experience with them was nice and friendly. I went almost every day in the summer and lots of times during the school year, during and after school. That was my escape from being treated mean to being accepted by total nice strangers. I've learned that people are good no matter how they dress or where they come from. So don't judge anyone unless you really know them.

Greetings from the beautiful Oregon coast! We have a slogan in our coastal county which proudly proclaims "Tillamook, the land of cheese, trees and ocean breeze." It should also include friendship.

It has been my good fortune to spend my entire life in this special part of the world. I found as a small child that most everyone in our community was surrounded by relatives. Not so with us. And that is why friends became very important in our lives. How fortunate for my three brothers and me that we learned true friendship is a strong bond which will last and influence you throughout your entire life.

Because of the isolation of our county (we have the Coast Range Mountains on the east and the Pacific Ocean on the west) we are quite often cut off by winter storms from the rest of western Oregon. Working together and the basis of true friendship has enabled us to solve many problems.

Fortunate am I to have been surrounded by friendship all my life. As I've grown older I appreciate even more the remarkable way in which friends give us compassion, faith and love.

Over the years friends and neighbors have given me fifty-two rosebushes. I knew every one of them by name and where they came from, but recently they suffered from blight and I lost them all. The memories have remained and I'm glad for that.

My son and his wife are teaching English in Croatia and they're making friends with people all over the world there. Both of them know how important friends are and that they can be found anywhere if we take the time to look.

129

I have been an employee of the U.S. Postal Service for twenty years. During those years I've met a lot of really nice people. Some have gone on to other things, such as retirement, unemployment, and there are those that have stayed. Many just passed briefly through my life; others "have left a footprint on my heart." Those I call my friends. We have endured many changes in the Postal Service. We have laughed, had some really good times, and some bad times. Watched each other's children grow up, suffered losses together, and shared some really bizarre phases.

I have a friend here that was having some really tough times and I worried about him. Well, I believe in angels. I gave him an angel pin to wear. This was many years ago and he still wears it to this day. Someone asked him about the pin, and his reply was that a dear friend gave the pin to him to help

him when he needed it most. He said he told people at his church about his extended family—us here at the Postal Service. And if you think about it we spend a good portion of our lives at work with these people. So yes I agree they are my extended family.

A really dear friend of mine at work suffered what to me would be the most difficult, a loss of a child in his prime of life. I did not know him but she asked me to do a music video of pictures of him for the funeral viewing. It was one the hardest things I've ever had to do. I felt her pain and sorrow. After seeing those pictures over and over I felt like he was part of my family. That is what friends do. I have shared countless times of laughter with this person. I love to hear her laugh and it pains me to see her suffer. But with the help of friends we seem to be able to make it through. Friends laugh together, cry together, share pain and happiness, because that's what we do.

I have also shared some really fun times with friends from my extended family. Short vacations that leave lasting impressions. And we share these often and love to laugh about them. Laughter is good for the soul.

We have a book of pictures that has evolved over the years, pictures of all the people we have worked with. We make copies and give them as a gift to those that retire. It is fun to look at those pictures and remember the times behind them.

My extended family, my friends at the Postal Service, they're all angels in disguise.

A true friend is…

…fiercely loyal.

…boundlessly loving.

…painstakingly patient.

…faultlessly forgiving.

…trustworthy without question.

…endlessly listening yet learning.

…understanding yet cautiously teaching and honestly corrective.

…discerning of the words you say.

…and those you don't.

…there for you, when you ask.

…and when you don't, but are in need.

…a rare possession, valued above all.

"*Your* friend is your needs answered," said Khalil Gibran. I realize that he meant more than in the material sense, but throughout my life the friends that I have met on the way have often manifested their friendship in thoughtful and kindly ways.

I have, many a time, found myself just outside p o v - e r t y ' s door, but when it seemed about to open a friend would hold it shut for me. In the early days in Africa this was often the case.

For example, one Christmas Eve, after many months without salary and the prospect of a meager Christmas, (bananas and dry kidney beans), I opened the back door to find a box on the step—inside, long untasted treats: tinned meat, Christmas pudding and Cadbury's chocolates!

When flown home to Scotland with a suspected brain tumor I found my bank account topped up by a friend "just in case it was needed."

That same friend some years later bought herself a ticket to Africa when I returned to make the ceremony to remove my Widows weeds so that I wouldn't have to go alone. She was afraid for my safety.

Since returning to Scotland new friends continue to surprise me with such

133

acts of generosity.

The cupboard has been empty, the house full. A knock at the door and a friend stands there, arms laden with groceries "as there were two for the price of one and I thought they might come in handy."

Or the postman delivers an inflatable bed ordered by the same thoughtful friend who knows that the family have all arrived for Christmas and the beds are too few.

The examples of friendship shown are many, from Lore who offered refuge when a family of eighteen became too much; Janet who was, and is, always there; Ndoh who lay beside me night after night when I cried for my husband and son; Susanna who brought shoes for the children when funds were low; Marla who made cake; Dot who put money in an envelope and popped it in my pocket; and Bob who entertained my visitors. These are friends from different countries, different cultures, but always with the same generosity of spirit.

Gibran also said on friendship that "your heart ceases not to listen to his heart." My friends have never ceased to listen to mine and I hope they have also heard its resounding gratitude.

I work with people who are addicted to opiates, or as one of the young people in the local academy where we hold weekly discussion sessions so eloquently put it earlier today, "Smack Heads."

I got into this line of work through meeting a woman called Dorothy who had a son addicted to heroin. I met her through my work with the local housing department in the highlands of Scotland.

The first time I met Dot she was dressing down a neighbor whose husband was selling her son prescription medication illegally. The second time she told me she wanted to form an organization called Alness Mothers Against Drugs, echoing the Cranhill Mothers Against Drugs movement in the East End of Glasgow who are famous for ousting all the dealers from their community. She was going through the experience of having an injecting heroin user, her son, living with her and wanted to make sure neither her community, nor other families would experience the distress she had witnessed firsthand.

I agreed to facilitate Dot in her objective, but confess I was more interested in keeping the level of empty houses down, preventing further loss of rental revenue and ultimately higher costs to the public purse than any high philanthropic ideal on my part.

However, I could not help myself from facilitating Dot's objective and was given permission by my manager to do so. Nobody could fail to be impressed by the sheer determination of this fifty-year young lady who possessed a rare personal quality that had the people she met gravitate toward her. Her will to prevent heroin from destroying her community took precedence over her own needs.

Dot was of pure mind and politically naive. I say was, because she's now three years further on, and has just decided to run for local counselor in the coming elections. Although still pure of mind, she is no longer politically naive. She has hurdled all the jumps placed before her including those placed in her way politically. She has had her eyes opened about how to make real structural changes, i.e. through political power. Of course my own reputation and experience have also been enhanced, making it potentially possible for me to project myself into the local political arena, something that I have always had an ambition to do!

Nevertheless, with Dot's decision to stand against the incumbent Councilor, I decided to put my own ambitions on hold and support Dorothy's election campaign. I put my own personal ambition to one side and put my energies into Dot because I believe in her goodness and believe she can win. She is one of my best friends.

How would I define friendship? As belief enough in someone to make you forego your own needs, for a while at least!

$\mathcal{I}$ used to see friendship as a child sees love from a parent: An unconditional gift I am given. If I came into contact with someone who didn't offer me that gift, I used to throw my walls up and say, "He is unfriendly; therefore he is no friend of mine."

As I mature, I see friendship more clearly as a parent sees love for a child: An unconditional gift I can give.

It does not matter how others may treat me. I have the power to be a friend to all people.

137

*I*t started on a plane full of exchange students bound for several countries in South America. I can remember trying to sleep and being awakened fairly regularly by one voice in particular. She was always loud and her speech was consistently vulgar. I'm sure I wasn't the only one thinking by the end of the trip that if she even ended up in the same country with me it would be too close.

About a month after settling in with my adopted family in Rio de Janeiro the phone rang. I can remember thinking as it did that if for some reason it was that girl from the plane I wanted whoever answered it to tell her I wasn't in. Why I sensed it would be her I'll never know—but it was. She had been asked to leave three separate placements in the Rio area. The director of the program had of necessity agreed to keep her in his home for the duration of her time in Brazil. Thus she ended up living in a luxury apartment facing Copacabana Beach, just a few blocks away from my more typical home.

I wasn't very good at lying, so after picking up the phone, when she suggested that we should get together, I couldn't think of any excuse at all. And that is how I met Micky. I can remember our first talk in my living room. It didn't take long for our conversation to get past the superficial level to where we were discussing matters and ideas of some depth and getting to know each other on a very personal level. I was stunned to find out how intelligent and insightful she was. It wasn't too long before I dared mention that some of her vocabulary was pretty tough on my ears and soul, and wondered if she could turn the use of expletives down a notch. She just laughed. I think it was just her way of playing with people—what we would now call yanking someone's chain—and she totally just dropped the act.

I won't go into too many details here but we were immediately fast friends and spend much of the remainder of our time together. My Brazilian family had requested an exchange student primarily to help their younger son learn English. They were going through some marital problems so I was pretty much on my own. That left lots of chances for Micky and me to come up with things to do together. We got to be pretty good getting around town. Though we might have been a bit too gutsy in some of our adventures, it was all harmless and fun. By the time we were to leave we had become almost inseparable. Sensing we might never see each other again, we stayed up for the last forty-eight hours straight—including the long flight back to Miami.

I never did see Micky again. We wrote for a while, always aware of the different directions into which our lives were heading. You see I was a Christian and Micky was Jewish. An odd pairing to be hanging out with a diverse group of African-Americans also placed in Rio, not to mention several people involved in the Brazilian film industry. If one of us was given any grief the other one was there to give support. We were a formidable pair. But I went on towards my career as a teacher. Micky became pretty active in the anti-establishment culture of the time. Eventually we lost touch. Though I've certainly remained closer to others or stayed in contact for longer periods of time, I know of few relationships that had more of an impact on who I've become.

I would never have chosen Micky as a likely candidate for friendship, but her

139

friendship found me. Over the years, it has pretty much been my experience that the people I've known the longest and whom I cherish the most are those with whom I don't have much in common. Ones I may initially have found grating or uninviting, but circumstances have put them in my path. It was my experience in Rio that taught me simply to say yes to friendship wherever it finds me.

Now when I look back I find my greatest riches to be the people I call friends. I am so grateful to have been able to learn from such a diverse group. Having taught high school for thirty years it may not be surprising that some of my heroes have been teenagers. Likewise, it's understandable that having parents who were older has meant that I love to associate with eighty-year-olds. Teaching now in a state prison it's probably a little more unexpected that I'm genuinely fond of some felons and have gained from watching the kindness, courage and character I've found there.

Just say yes to new opportunities, then open your heart to the people you meet along the way.

Look for strengths they have that you may lack and learn from the example.

Be especially anxious to take advantage of the treasure of meeting someone from a different background or culture for what they can teach you that enriches your life, broadens your understanding and increases your ability to reach out to others.

It's a simplistic formula, I know, but I was fortunate to learn it while young and it has served me well. It is this experience with friendship that has brought me great joy—so I share it.

A friend is not just an acquaintance. Not just a stranger who gave you a helping hand in time of need. A friend is someone who has taken the time to know you. A friend knows what your dreams are and isn't afraid to hold you to your commitments. A friend truly listens to you and understands who you are. A friend helps you to understand what your potential really is. A friend wants to protect you, even if that means protecting you from yourself.

I have many acquaintances who I like to be around and that I'm very close to, but few people have reached the status of a true friend. The two top people on my list of friends are my father and mother. They are the embodiment of the word 'friend' in my eyes.

141

In 1958 when I ran away from my home in the highlands of Scotland I left behind me not only grinding poverty, but also the companionship of my brothers and sisters. It was to be many years before any meaningful contacts would be made again. We met on a few occasions, but I always felt a stranger, the one who somehow had broken the rules. While my life was filled with travel, because the man I married was in the services, the farthest my sisters moved was to the place of my mother's birth, Shropshire on the English-Welsh border.

It was about fifteen years ago, with my marriage over and my children grown, that my love for the land of my birth brought me home again. I longed to know where I really belonged, and the need to find my roots led me into genealogy, which is where my real friendship with my sisters began.

My Scottish side is well documented in the local records, but my English-Welsh side proved much harder. This is where I turned to my sisters for help. I was tentative at first, not knowing how they themselves felt about the past, but as we started to talk about our mother's family we became bonded in ways I had never thought possible. We traveled up and down the roads of our mother's childhood, sharing all manner of things about our lives. We found the houses she had lived in with her family, sometimes we talked to the people living in them now. Through this we have met many people interested in what we're doing.

Always I'm looking for a clearer record of my grandfather, Tom Jones, killed in a mine disaster, but it is a common name in Wales, and I need to be certain I have the right one. Through my search I have found my ancestors, people who lived and loved, had children of their own, walked these villages and lanes as I do now.

I will always be grateful to Tom Jones as my search for him has led me back to my sisters and a friendship which gives me knowledge of belonging again, a certainty of peace and value. I trust and am trusted. I know we will weather any storm life may wish to throw at us. As we continue to search for our roots we are planting our own roots of love even deeper.

A friend knows when to stay loyally in the supporting cast, even if invited to accept a starring role.

In May of 1945, World War II, I was in the 474th Infantry Regiment, attached to General Patton's 3ʳᵈ Army. We had just finished our combat duties in Belgium during the Battle of the Bulge Campaign, when our unit, listed as "Task Force A," was sent to Drammen, Norway. We were a part of the Norwegian Liberation Forces. It would be another five months before we could go back to the United States.

Shortly after our arrival, I met a girl and was taken in by the Lonjer family. From the beginning I was treated as one of their own. I had never been away from home before, and the traditional Norwegian meals and care they gave me were very much appreciated, especially since my unit had been living on K and C rations.

Inger and I became sweethearts. I was nineteen and she was eighteen. We hiked along the fjords, climbed the mountains and enjoyed the countryside. Her older brother George was always with us, acting as chaperone. But as close as we were, time and space separated us after the war.

Many years later, in 1990, I was traveling in Drammen and decided to step into the tourist office. I mentioned to the lady standing behind the desk that I had been there during the war.

We started to talk and when I wrote Inger's name on a piece of paper, the women glanced at it and screamed, "That is my best friend!" After a few phone calls I met Inger, her husband,

145

and the remaining family in Asker, Norway. It was easy to re-kindle a friendship of forty years ago. We had a glorious time, looking at photographs of our teen romance and talking and visiting. This was very much a highlight of my twenty years of overseas global travels. A friendship I'll never forget. We are living in perilous times. Things have changed, but relationships are always important.

146

Fifty years ago two young children became friends. Nothing remarkable in that, one could say. They played together, giggled about things, whispered together about excitement and discovery, shared secrets and got into scrapes together. If one was around, rest assured the other wasn't far away. In every way they enjoyed each other's company.

Through the years other friends came and went, but a special bond kept these two girls very close. They shared confidences about little things like gossip and beauty secrets, and big things like romance and heartbreak. They always had one another to turn to. By this time there was nothing they didn't know about each other, and trust grew for both kindness and confidence.

Even when marriage to their respective partners took place and they were separated by five hundred miles there was still a special bond between them. In time they exchanged photographs of each other's children, wrote fairly often, spoke twice a year on the telephone when it was their birthdays and met very occasionally, as money was scarce.

When one of them got divorced the other stood by her and helped her through it. Now they are sending photographs of their grandchildren to each other and write more often, and the conversations are a lot of laughter, and 'do you remember when we…'

That friendship grew from liking to loving, trusting and being loyal. I should know, as I'm one of those children. I treasure my friendship with Eleanor very much and thank God often that Eleanor and I met fifty years ago.

147

*A*my was my friend. She helped me through times when I was confused and down, that's what a real friend does. She would only question me enough to find out what she needed to so she could help me. I remember a time when I needed to move and all she drove was a little white Datsun and I had all this big furniture, lamps etc. And we stuck it in her car and drove it to my new place. She would help without question, she was the strong one. We would stay up late hours talking and just hanging out deciding what we would do over the weekend.

I have a friend till this day that loves and cares about me. This friend took me in when I really needed someone. I was going to have a baby, and she and her family took me into their home and took me to church and doctor's appointments. That's when I truly needed someone in my life because I

was placing this baby for adoption. You feel lonely and scared and confused. Candie is very strong and a smart person. She has been in my life for about eight years; in fact she lives close by. I still see her and her family.

I remember finding little notes on my bed after coming from the doctor's office or some other occasion. She went with me to the hospital and she was there helping me along, after the baby was born. We drove around until I was calm enough to go back to their home. We drove for a long time I remember. She helped me get through that time. Candie allowed me to stay with them while I went to cosmetology school. I've never forgotten the kindness she showed me. No matter what decisions I've made in my life I know she won't judge me and that she still loves me. When I finished school she gave me a wonderful party with her famous cinnamon rolls. On my birthday she brought cinnamon rolls for my whole class to eat. What a nice surprise. She has been a wonderful angel in my life. She allowed me to start a new life and have a skill I can use to survive in this big world.

I wrote in my journal once to express my gratitude for the friends that have crossed my path.

Tracy Lynn Steabril was the very first friend I ever had. We used to have sleepovers at her grandma's house. We used flashlights under the covers so her grandma wouldn't hear us because we giggled and laughed and talked until morning. Tracy would come and visit me from San Diego—we were eleven years old. We would play outside on the playground and swing and swing and laugh. She made me forget what my real home life was like. She can still make me smile, with her long blond hair, her blue eyes and her funny looking feet.

Can you imagine having a friend that can make you laugh and smile so much that you can forget all that hurts inside? She was just that kind of friend. She could smile and boy could she swing high—but what else can you remember when you are eleven. I miss her—I hope someday she'll know just how much she meant to me, because she doesn't know it, but she helped me to be happy and free for the little while she was my friend.

NANCY HOPKINS
MEDICAL TRANSPORT DRIVER

If you should have the fortune to have a
good friend, a friend whom you treasure, then
let them know. Why should tender words
never be said of such until they're gone!

150

At 5:30 a.m. I lie in my warm bed and listen to the sound of wind chimes outside my window. The digital clock on the nightstand silently switches to 5:31. In nine minutes the alarm will remind me it's time to get up. Time to greet the canyon breezes that try to serenade me back to sleep. It's time to meet my friends for our morning run. The weather man warned it would be cold and the wind will make it colder. My muscles are asking for a day off but I know that my friends will be waiting for me at 6:00.

As I watch the clock flip to 5:32 I think about warmer weather and the birds that sing to us some beautiful spring mornings. My friends and I laugh at the chickadees calling out to each other from the tops of the blue spruces. We talk about our children who are growing up, leaving elementary school, starting high school, graduating, going

to college, getting married. We celebrate grandchildren being born. We discuss our plans for some summer vacations with our families. When summer finally arrives we leave earlier in the morning so that we can beat the heat. As we dodge the paperboy making his rounds we marvel at beautifully landscaped flower gardens. We talk about different varieties of plants we've each tried to grow and plan our own gardens. We verbally redecorate many of the homes we run past with new doors ("Lose the purple paint!"), new roof lines, or shutters.

It's 5:34. I think about autumn mornings in the mountains. I remember the magical moments we've spent together marveling at the sight of golden aspen leaves sprinkling the dark pine trees like rose petals. Running along trails that have been carpeted with orange and gold, we've heard elk bugling

151

and watched eagles glide silently overhead. We talk about how beautiful the world is and how lucky we are to be here at this moment. How blessed we are to be healthy. How grateful we are to have each other. We've shared more spectacular sunrises than most people will ever see. We've shared secrets and sorrows. I know that everything I confide to these women will stay just between us. The rhythm we fall into as our feet move along the pavement says it all. When we run together we are one. We've been there for each other through illness and injury. We've laughed and cried together. We've supported each other through good times and bad. Without these women I could not have made it through the long illness and death of my father. They have been my counselors and my confidants.

It's 5:38 and in two minutes I'll hear a collage of Spanish, static, and golden oldies blasting away from the alarm. The wind chimes are just barely tinkling. Maybe it won't be that cold. I love calm winter mornings when the stars sparkle overhead and unplowed roads are calling for our footprints. The moon is so bright we see our shadows running ahead of us. Sometimes we don't talk when we run. We just share the experience in silent gratitude.

At 5:39 I turn off the alarm and I force myself to leave the comfort of my electric blanket and crawl out of bed. It's time to get ready. My friends will be waiting.

$\mathcal{N}$elson De Mille said that, "We are all pilgrims on the same journey—but some pilgrims have better road maps." And once in a while we need someone else to help us with the map reading.

During a sudden torrential downpour in Moscow, Russia, two friends and I ran for shelter. Our way into a nearby church was blocked by a substantial pool that had collected at the gated entrance. Without any hesitation, my friend Sergey stepped into the water, which came well above his ankles, and carried me to higher ground.

What makes his gift all the more remarkable is that Sergey, not being a rich man, was wearing the only pair of shoes he owned. He is one of the heroes of the everyday who teach the profound lessons and help us reach our potential.

Nancy Lindemeyer, former editor-in-chief of *Victoria* magazine, describes such individuals in her editorial "In Praise of Pathfinders": "It takes days and years to bring us to a place of tranquility, and often it is through the assistance of others that we see the road ahead and make all the right turns. My own journey has not always been smooth, but I have been lucky to find those more sure-footed to give me guidance and direction."

Insights can come from unexpected sources. A few years ago I had the privilege of raising a fledgling robin that had fallen out of its nest high up in a pine tree. While observing my futile efforts to return the bird to its home, a neighbor commented, "Well, a cat is sure to get that one." Not liking his statement, I decided that a cat would not get this one.

It took the continuous efforts of family and friends to keep the young bird's appetite

153

satisfied. We named her Niblia, the Georgian word for robin. In a short time, our fledgling trusted us and her new surroundings. She and I became friends on her terms. I could always count on her to be just a few feet away when I was outside weeding or planting. On warm summer days, Niblia enjoyed baths in our garden. Many an afternoon she would scold me if I neglected to fill her small, nasturtium-rimmed pool with water. Until she grew old enough to be on her own, she spent the nights indoors in a cardboard box equipped for her needs.

Parenting efforts went well until one day, returning home during a sudden severe windstorm, I found my robin on the patio hanging on for dear life to a dried-out, broken-off twig. Not speaking bird language, I had been unable to teach my feathered charge the difference between a dead twig and the life-saving strength of a living branch.

I immediately picked her up and made sure that she was all right. Secure once more, Niblia soon fell asleep, nestled in my palm. She recovered and returns every spring to build a nest close to her own beginnings.

The twig experience had an interesting effect. It made me reexamine the beliefs and causes to which I had given my allegiance. Were they anchored to something sustainable or were they attached to something frail and flimsy? Was I entrusting myself to a dead twig or to a living branch? And did I stand by a cause because I still had faith in it or because I had once believed in it?

Those were questions I learned to ask myself now and then. A feathered friend had taught me an important lesson.

DSP

$\mathcal{P}$ersonally I believe that friendship, and the lessons we learn together over the course of a lifetime are our biggest assets. The wisdom, happiness, and humility gained through sharing your thoughts and feelings with a true friend are blessings I hope we all endeavor to obtain.

The friendless man awakes once more,

He sees the dark waves before him

Seabirds bathing with wings spread

As snow and frost blend with falling hail.

Then are of the wounds of his heart bitter…

—The Wanderer

*W*hen this poem was first recited those listening would have easily understood the depth of this man's despair. It was composed over a thousand years ago, in Anglo-Saxon England. That society was built upon ties of family and friendship. From the smallest village to the courts of the kings, people relied on friends in times of need. With no fire departments, no police, no Red Cross, the ability to survive a disaster depended on how many friends were nearby.

Throughout most of medieval Europe,

a person accused in a criminal case was doomed without friends to stand up for him. This was not an empty gesture. If the accused were judged guilty, his friends could also receive the judgment. In many cases, this was not death or imprisonment, but exile. It was assumed that the one convicted would not last long without the protection of his friends. There are many stories, both historical and fictional, of the fate of the exile and those who chose to join him.

But there was another side to the

medieval concept of friendship. Often the penalty set for a crime was for the guilty person to be sent on a pilgrimage of atonement. Again, it was likely that he wouldn't survive the journey. However, if he did and returned to his home, he was taken back with forgiveness. This is something that I at first found difficult to understand. People who had confessed to theft, betrayal, even murder were accepted and forgiven once their exile was over.

Today we still rely on our friends to be there in times of need, to believe in us. But how many of us have the kind of friendship that would share a journey of expiation? And which of us could, when the exile returned repentant, forgive and trust him as before?

I don't know if I have that sort of friend. I don't know if I could be that sort of friend. I do know that a thousand years ago people believed that this is what a friend was.

157

I am very blessed. I have known my best friend Anna since we attended nursery together almost forty years ago. We went through some childhood jealousies but our temperamental differences gradually became a source of strength in our friendship. Anna liked coming around for my mom's English home cooking and what she called 'normality' and I was fascinated by the exotic artistic flavor that ran through her house. This included my first taste of garlic and eating raw onions on toast while her mom sang operatic arias!

The most endearing quality that Anna possesses is her ability to be non-judgmental. She has always been there for me. When my three-year-old son Callum was hit by a car just days before Christmas, Anna was the one person who offered to abandon her family's Christmas arrangements and leave her young children to travel six hundred miles to hold my hand why

we waited for news of Callum's prognosis. In shock, I was paralyzed by indecision and asked her to wait by the phone.

Surrounded by dedicated medical staff in Intensive Care, my husband and newborn daughter, it was the loneliest Christmas ever. A strange statement for a Buddhist to make, but no one wants to spend that time of year in hospital, a hundred miles from home. Anna listened patiently on the phone, prayed and never once blamed me for the accident for which I felt responsible.

Another friend, Seymour, who lived closer to the hospital, brushed aside my inability to ask for support and sensing that I was the one most in need, announced he would take me away from the hospital to which I had become welded for a week. We had a cheerful lunch where he listened and I tried to come to terms with Callum's injuries.

Thankfully he made a complete physical recovery, though emotionally he is still healing. I later found out that by coming to support me in my hour of need, Seymour had foregone the opportunity to see his dying father for the last time. He was already complete and excepting of his father's passing and had no regrets.

The Dalai Lama talks about the main theme of Buddhism being altruism based on compassion and love. My friends selflessly put my welfare and happiness before their own needs and desires. They did not stop to think what they were 'doing'. They were just 'being' with my suffering, and through their kindness they expressed deep compassion, without judgment and blame.

Anna is always there, wherever she lives in the world and however often we communicate. I can be who I am and know that even when I make mistakes she totally accepts me, gently guiding me so I can forgive myself. Our deep connection and understanding of each other's humanity allows us to express our love unconditionally and for that I am eternally grateful.

It all started when I turned sixteen years old and I bought a scooter. Later I wanted something better and took my dad to look at a British motorcycle, a 500 cc single cylinder. At that time the only good bikes were Harley-Davidson's and British bikes. My dad said that "If you are going to buy a motorcycle you need to get a Harley-Davidson."

I could not believe he would let me get a big bike, but the next day I went to the Harley-Davidson dealership and found a used 56 FLH HD.

After a while I got to be friends with the mechanic at the dealership and he asked if I would be interested in joining the motorcycle club; I did and what a bunch of nice people they were. At age sixteen I was the only unmarried member, but they accepted me and treated me real nice. I had very good trips and a lot of fun till I was drafted in the Army. After my hitch in the Army I went back to the motorcycle club. It was as if I had never left. A little while later I moved to Utah and joined another club and also a British motorcycle club. In both I have made long-lasting friendships, because when you meet another biker there is an automatic connection, a camaraderie. We share, have a good time, see the sights and enjoy the freedom riding a bike brings. Right now I have eight bikes. I like to work on them. Bikers are known to be big-hearted. They are some of the most charitable groups in the country and raise hundreds of thousands of dollars every year. As long as I can remember, I've always tried to pick good people and it paid off.

Vedo l'amico come uno specchio davanti al quale posso pensare ad alta voce, proprio perchè è l'unico vero individuo nel quale mi riconosco.

Il sorriso dell'amico è una finestra che si apre nel mio intimo, la sua parola è espressione di quel che amo e spero.

Il suo abbraccio è la sincera accoglienza di un cuore che rispetta e ama.

Gli amici che accompagnano la mia vita e che conoscono i miei difetti, sono gli unici ai quali posso francamente parlare delle mie qualità.

Credo nell'amico che mi cammina a fianco e nell'eloquenza dei suoi silenzi.

I believe a friend to be like a reflection in a mirror, in front of which I can think aloud because he is the only individual in whom I can always recognize myself. The smile of a friend is a window, which opens into the deepest part of my soul; his words are the real expressions of what I admire and trust.

His warm hold is the truthful welcome of a heart which respects and loves.

The friends I share my life with, those who know my weaknesses, are the only ones with whom I can openly talk about who I am.

I believe in the friend who walks by my side, and in the expression of his silence.

161

In the world of ballet, for pupils who want to learn the real meaning and spirit of dance, there's only one way, and that is to find the right teacher. This is not just a matter of finding someone who has skill and knowledge and is perhaps a great dancer or choreographer, but one who has a deeper understanding with you, and can convey to you the spirit of the dance.

I did not begin to study ballet until I was eighteen, when I was considered an "old man!" I initially went as part of my physical therapy, after an accident. I had several teachers. From some I learned the basics and the discipline. I was told simply, "You have no choice, you learn or you go!"

I met Rudolf Nureyev a number of times, and even had a lesson with him. Nureyev was a brilliant man, but it was Gilbert Canova who formed with me that great and subtle bond of artistic friendship through which I discovered rhythm within. For this one needs no music, because the soul of the dance is inside, even as one walks along a street.

For me Canova made the ballet room where we worked a spiritual place — one different from any other, where I felt happy, and full of positive energy. If a dancer does not feel this, he's in the wrong place.

There are many excellent teachers of dance, but the great secret is to find the person with whom you have that unique bond so that in the heart of movement you are one. It is a friendship like no other, a way in which you are given a gift every day for the rest of your life.

When I lost my husband I became a recluse. Then one day a friend told me that everyone has a cross to bear. She was right and I decided to change.

Now when I go somewhere people say, "Here comes the merry widow." In the past I have been a sad person. Now I have a number of friends and life is good again.

163

I was a soldier once, during those turbulent 1960s when the Vietnam War tested true friendship. I grew up with this person, and shared all of the rights of passage that young men blunder through. That is until the war. As teenagers leaving the nest of high school, I chose the military and he chose the opposition.

This person became embroiled in the anti-war movement with a passion. He grew his hair long and became a card-carrying member of the anti-war counterculture. In other words, the complete antithesis of my own persona.

I had chosen another path. My path led me into the morass of the war with what I thought of as patriotic zeal. Years passed, and we remained on opposite sides of the issue; the issue that was characterized by mutual loathing of the other's position.

Except for this person. You see, even though we were exponents of diametrically political positions, he still had the time to correspond with his "misguided" childhood mate who spent years in Vietnam, and never proselytized about the issue. All his letters were about things that would be of interest to someone in my position: mutual friends, weddings, girls, music and never about things that would divide us.

After many years in the War, I came home to a country that had changed for men like me. The protesters had won; men in uniform were spat upon. So it was with a bit of trepidation that I flew back to my hometown, defiantly in uniform. My friend had agreed to meet me at the airport and I got the welcome I wanted: just a good old-fashioned greeting between old friends.

*Friends share the ceremony of life. They
also give each other space when necessary.*

Trips to a zoo to see elephants, seals, and polar bears, "Girls night out" to go bowling in costumes; catching dinner and a movie. Going dancing until midnight or later, slumber parties where favorite movies are watched all night long. Vacations to Disneyland, Disney World, the Grand Canyon, Zion National Park, Yellowstone, and a nearby festival. Attending Van Gogh art exhibits in Chicago, Washington, D.C. and Los Angeles. Going to Seattle for a weekend, to Hawaii for a wedding, and of course the beach. These are just some of the great adventures I've had with my friends.

A friend will recognize a look or gesture and quickly know what I'm thinking. I can say a phrase or a sentence that will bring back memories of laughter or tears that are then shared again. They'll go to a party just because I want to. Give me a ride home when I miss the bus. I'll postpone an outing if a babysitter can't be found. We'll make sure the other is aware of and invited to upcoming activities. They'll come over when I don't feel like going out. We like the same movies for different reasons. Different guys for the same reasons. We are individuals with our own tastes and opinions. They accept me as I am, not expecting any more than I'm willing to give.

My friends have allowed me to share in some of the fabulous moments in their lives. I get to be an aunt to their children and another daughter to their parents. I've attended weddings, birthday parties, plays, baptisms, and funerals. I was even present for the birth of one's firstborn son. We share in each other's joys and sorrows, in the successes and the disappointments. "I told you so" is rarely heard and a shoulder is always there to lean on. And more often than not, help is offered before we can even ask for it.

Friends can be like family. Family members can be friends. Being a military chaplain's daughter, I've lived in various places and left behind many friends. But the memory of how they each blessed my life will always be with me. With every friend I make, my family circle grows. Each of my friends has qualities which make them unique to me, share talents and skills that broaden my horizons. My friends make me want to be a better person. They help me to be a better person. My friends are some of the best people I know and I love each of them dearly. I will always try to be as great a friend to each of them as they are to me. The world is full of potential friends. Friendship can ignore race, religion, background, and upbringing. Reach out your hand and see who grabs hold. I can be defined by the friends I have. We all can.

We have been making violins in Cremona for centuries. The greatest master of all was Antonio Stradivari (1648-1737), and I have a life-sized statue of him in the entrance to my workshop. A recent visitor remarked that she thought I looked like him. I told her that Stradivari was a tall man, over six feet, and he had two wives and ten children. I'm only a small man, and am happy with one wife and five children.

My four sons have all followed me into the old Cremonesi art, which we have renewed again in the last century. It takes over two hundred hours of handwork to create a violin, and all the varnishes are made on the premises from natural ingredients imported from all over the world. A violin is of great beauty to the eye as well as the ear, and will last for centuries, growing better all the time if it is cared for properly.

It is not coincidence that a violin is shaped like the body of a woman. Its voice is the most human of instruments, and no two are the same even if they are made from the same inner mold. When someone asks me to make a violin for them I have formed the ability to judge them and see into their hearts, to learn to know them.

It is a unique art of friendship that I will create with my hands an instrument upon which they will play the music that is within themselves, and both of us will have joy in it.

Often I think that the most powerful expressions of friendship come not from those you know to be your friends, but from strangers who, briefly crossing your path, offer an act of kindness that is as powerful as love, and gives an example of our own greatest potential.

As a young comedian, aged just eighteen, my girlfriend Angie (now my wife of twenty-three years and my best friend) and I were invited to leave Australia and travel to Germany to become part of a show that was being put together for a club in Munich. We knew nothing, as you don't when you're only eighteen. We were told to buy two one-way tickets to Germany. The promoters putting the show together would then reimburse the money we had spent (which was just about all we had to our names) when we got there, as well as buy the return portion of the air tickets for us. So armed with nothing but our wits (so virtually nothing), Angie and I headed for Germany. I had traveled quite regularly as a child, having a father in the Navy, but Angie had not been on a plane until we flew together.

Suddenly, the two of us were in the middle of a new country, unable to speak the language apart from some broken school German, and with very little money. At least we would get paid once we started work. We arrived in Munich, only to find that the show had collapsed and nothing was going to happen. More than that, there was no way any recovery of moneys already laid out would be met, let alone return tickets to Australia.

Someone who was involved in the show's original negotiations took pity on the two of us and gave us a job driving around Munich 'sniping' posters onto old walls and

169

construction sites for up-and-coming pop acts that were touring Europe. 'The Police' I recall was one of the bands struggling to make a name for themselves. In return for getting up at three a.m. each morning to do this, we were given an old van to drive around in and lodgings.

Our accommodation was a small single room up ten flights of stairs, without bathroom, and an old mattress on the floor. There was no money and we felt even worse as we grew more tired and hungry. Every couple of days Angie would get her toiletries together and walk four blocks to a public bathroom. For a few pfennig she at least was able to have a shower and feel like a human being.

Angie was becoming more and more stressed and weary, hungry and scared as days turned into weeks. One morning she walked the four blocks to the public baths,

only to find them closed. She slumped into a pile and burst into tears right there on the street. She was tired and dirty, and had reached the end of her ability to cope. As she sat there in the middle of a Munich city square crying, she heard a soft German male voice. She looked up with tears rolling down her face to see a handsome and very smartly dressed young man standing above her. When she said that she understood very little German, he began to speak to her in English.

He asked if there was anything he could do. Helping her up, he offered a hand-kerchief to wipe her face. For some reason, Angie sensed some kindness in this stranger's eyes and began to talk to him. He walked with her a couple of blocks, and as I was on my way to meet Angie, unaware that this had transpired, we suddenly found ourselves on the same corner. Angie introduced this man as Echardt, and I shook his hand. As it was approaching lunchtime, he suggested that if we were hungry (ravenous would be a better description) we might like to join him for some lunch at a little place nearby. We were soon having the best meal we'd had in quite some time. After lunch, he said he had to go but gave us his business card and said if we ever needed anything, to call him.

It turned out that at the age of just thirty-four, Echardt was a highly successful businessman, a millionaire owner of a number of large chiropractic establishments throughout Germany. For the next few weeks a wonderful and deeply moving relationship developed as this man opened his luxury home to us to come over and "have a bath," watch television and for a brief time feel normal again. He would take us out to dinner whenever we looked hungry. On one occasion we bumped into him in the City district. After finding out that we had nothing to do, he piled us into his Porsche and drove us to the airport, where he took us for an afternoon in his private plane, (he piloted the small four seater aircraft) for a tour of Bavaria, around some of the castles, and then eventually back to Munich. It seemed almost bizarre that two young people, who had nothing, could suddenly find themselves flying around German skies in a private plane.

Despite life becoming one hundred percent better after meeting this man, Angie and I were starting to get run down from the whole ordeal. Echardt could see this too, and one night while having dinner at his house, he asked how much money we thought we needed to get over this "hump." We had been trying to save enough money to get to England so I could get some work performing comedy before an English-speaking audience. After telling him how much was needed, he asked us to come by his office the following day. When we did, he handed us an envelope with enough money for the trip to England.

From that moment on we didn't look back. We got a job in a show on the Isle of Man, earned enough to buy tickets home, and four months later, were safe on familiar soil.

Had it not been for the kindness of this man, who knows what could have happened. It was this friendship shown by a stranger that causes us to this day, some twenty-four years later, to have some barometer by which to measure our own actions. I'll leave the last words to Angie, where this moment of compassion started.

Echardt... there are no words to describe him. I honestly believe he was an angel. And I was touched by him. Every time I think of him, to this day, there is a thought that takes me back to God. When I recall how he touched my grubby, ugly tear-streaked face that first day, well it was an epiphany, to say the least.

I've often tried to find Echardt over the years, to thank him and give him back his money—but I've never been able to trace him. But I know this to be true—what we give out comes back to us in turn. So I know kindness and friendship are bound to have followed him all the days of his life. And Echardt, now approaching sixty, if you happen to be reading this book—thank you for the friendship you showed to two lost Australians all those years ago.

173

My brother Ron and I did just about everything together. Only a year apart in age, we played, we laughed, we got into mischief and we sometimes got into trouble. We often argued and fought with each other, but even after our many scuffles and disagreements the fighting was always quickly forgotten and life continued as if nothing had happened. We never held grudges. As the big brother I often worried about Ron and in my earliest recollections of our youth I remember feeling an urgent need to watch out for him. Perhaps I felt it to be my duty as the older brother and I was proud of this responsibility.

I was eight years old and in the third grade, Ron was seven and in the second grade. We always took the same route home from school, and usually without any consequence. But when spring came that year, it brought with it a couple of sixth-grade bullies who began to follow us each day. The bullying started with name-calling and soon escalated to shoving and a few threats. I was concerned for Ron, but since most of the action seemed to be directed towards me it didn't bother me too much.

One day, perhaps it was because I wouldn't bend to their taunting and demands, the two young bullies pushed me to the ground; one boy held onto my left foot, the other boy twisted the right foot. I was certain it was done with the intention of making me cry, but I refused to give them the satisfaction. Although I was only eight years old, I had felt the sting of a punch and the thud of a kick before, and for some reason I wasn't fearful for myself at that instance as I frantically looked for my brother to see if he was being handled in any way.

My eyes froze on him. His eyes were

dazed, there seemed to be a slight tremble as he stood there. At first I thought that perhaps he was afraid they were going to hurt him too, but then I realized, he wasn't concerned for himself; he was saying a prayer for me. I watched him, his eyes opened and tears welled up inside. Fear was upon him as he frantically looked everywhere for someone to help his brother. He searched the ground for something he could use to strike these two young tormentors. Then, as all this was taking place in an open field within shouting distance of several homes, Ron spotted a lady who had just turned to see what was going on. Ron shouted for her to run, please run to us. His fervent prayer was answered.

This wonderful lady, perhaps the mother of a young child herself, came to my rescue, pulled these boys away and gave them a scolding they wouldn't soon forget. Ron tearfully asked if I was okay. When I said yes, he smiled and said "That was pretty cool how that lady came over and helped you." I acted like it was no big deal but inside I knew. I knew that my little brother, my friend, was watching out for me and had saved me from a good beating.

He looked out for me that day. I hope he knows that I have always tried to look out for him. That's what friends and brothers do. Recently, Ron indicated to me that he's doing fine and didn't need me to watch out for him right now but to keep an eye on his little ones and wife. Ron passed away suddenly a year ago and I dedicate these thoughts of our friendship to his family.

With love, Uncle Ray

175

MEGAN GOODRICH
STUDENT, JUNIOR HIGH SCHOOL

There is nothing more important than friends. Nothing can compare to a good friendship. People in your life may come and go, but as long as you have one or two special relationships you can do anything.

176

Index

Members Worldwide Adidas Organization 6
Anderson, Douglas 155
Arundel, Liz 158
Batchelor, Joie 60
Baxter, Stewart 135
Beaman, Nesta 147
Bedore, Laura 42
Bernard, James 119
Bilbao, Josefa 163
Bissolotti, Francesco 168
Bocelli, Andrea 161
Bothmer, Carmen von 94
Brady, Suzanne 144
Brewer, Cindie L. 20
Brown, Norman 17
Cage, J. Chris 62
Calder, Penny Ritchie 78
Campbell, Kevin 48
Castroman, Nicole H. 77
Cavin, Karen 138
Chen, Shuying 46
Christiansen, Andrea 19
Christie, Lisa 41
Clark, Linda 148
Connell, Jo Ann 105
Coutts, Danny 103
Cremonesi, Antonella 39
D'Aleo, Alessandro 162

Davis, Meg 22
Davy, Mildred 129
Dent, Kevin 104
Disraeli, Benjamin 82
Douglas, Hanna 57
Drozda, Paulette F. 112
Dusserre, Beverly 44
Espinoza, Paul 65
Fassbender, Lee 145
Frogley, Janet 132
Gilfillan, John D. 126
Goodall, Jane 9
Goodrich, Megan 176
Graham, Reverend Billy 61
Hack, Ron 160
Hatch, Très 1, 29
Heston, Charlton 68
Hopkins, Nancy 150
Hoskisson, Elizabeth 79
Huber, Elaine 36
Hulme, Jonathan 96
Itoe, Anne 133
Jack, Elaine L. 101
Jones, Kirsten P. 165
Keddington, Dorothy M. 99
Lansdale, Joe R. 107
MacDonald, Megan 142
Mackay, Catherine 58
Mackenzie, John 117
Madsen, Ronald E. 35
Martinez, Ray 174
Medina, Maggie 64

Meer, Jeffrey 110
Merrow, Jane 80
Mikeladze, Natia 81
Miller, Dr. Kim 106
Mori, Irene Mano 13
Morris, Britain C. 137
Morrison, Dr. Alexander B. 27
Mtchedlishvili, Marina 47
Neal, Kaleigh 38
Newman, Sharan 156
Nielsen, Karen 166
Nimmagudda, Neha 123
Oldroyd, Susan E. 151
Pearson, Carol Lynn 111
Perry, Anne 74
Peters, Barbara 30
Pezzani, Seba 114
Platt, Doris S. 16, 49, 71, 83, 121, 153
Randazzo, Arlene 100
Rich, Dustin 141
Seal, Kent M. 3
Sharifi, Sayed Ahmad 32
Spencer, Jim 108
Stauffer, Judy 23
Stewart, Tina 26
Terzian, Vera 95
Thomas, Helen 7
Vanblaircum, Norma 130
Vianes, Abbie 4
Wiesel, Elie 37
Williams, Angie 173
Williams, Scott 169